LEO ORNSTEIN
PIANO WORKS, 1913-1990

WITH AN INTRODUCTION BY
MICHAEL BROYLES AND DENISE VON GLAHN

FOREWORD BY SEVERO ORNSTEIN

DOVER PUBLICATIONS, INC.
MINEOLA, NEW YORK

Copyright

Copyright © 2012 by The Estate of Leo Ornstein
Foreword © 2012 by Severo Ornstein
Introduction © 2012 by Michael Broyles and Denise Von Glahn
All rights reserved.

Bibliographical Note

This Dover edition, first published in 2012, is a new compilation of music by Leo Ornstein, originally published between 1913 and 1990. Most of the music has been newly engraved by Severo Ornstein. Impressions of the Thames, Wild Men's Dance, and Impressions of Chinatown have been reprinted from early authoritative editions.

International Standard Book Number

ISBN-13: 978-0-486-49077-9
ISBN-10: 0-486-49077-7

Manufactured in the United States by Courier Corporation
49077701
www.doverpublications.com

Contents

Foreword

The piano seems to be going most of the time; that's what I notice as an infant. Later on, I'm sitting beside my father on the piano bench as he practices. Two piles of matches are on the music stand. Each time he repeats a passage, I move a match from one pile to the other. Sometimes the passage repeats seamlessly; I listen carefully to note where it starts over.

The many kinds of music he plays all make sense to me, each piece telling its own story. Only many years later do I discover that pianists can tell the story badly with misplaced emphasis or tempo—can even hit wrong notes that jar the ear.

At some point I begin to recognize the sound of my father's own music. "It sounds Chinesey, doesn't it?" he says to me one day. I don't know what he's playing—A La Chinoise perhaps, or maybe something new he's writing.

His temperament is as volatile as the music he writes. We're in his studio, deep in the woods on a New Hampshire hillside. Earlier he was practicing some Beethoven, but now he's shouting at my mother, his faithful scribe, seated nearby at a card table, pencil poised over some manuscript paper. He's frustrated because he can't remember how he got from point A to point B in the piece he's writing. A moment ago, as the music poured out through his fingers, the transition was smooth and natural. Now he's reduced to mere skill in building a bridge, and he's dissatisfied with the alternatives he's coming up with. None is as good, in his judgment, as the one that came with the initial flow of inspiration.

Another day we're rushing home from swimming in the river from which we kids have been unceremoniously yanked. Our father is singing, punctuating his voice with random syllables as we tear along. A musical idea has occurred to him and he is desperately trying to remember it until he can get to a pencil and paper where he can write it down.

"You can't shoehorn every idea into the same style," he says in response to the observation that his music is extremely varied. "Every idea demands its own style, its own idiom." He's disdainful of the modern preoccupation with style and with novelty, per se. "It's substance that matters. No amount of novelty can disguise or compensate for its absence. Most composers would give their right arm for a good tune," he says. He describes some music as "treading water."

When I retired in 1984, I decided to rescue my father's music from the neglect into which he had allowed it to sink over the fifty years since he had been a star proponent of modern music, including his own. Over the ensuing two decades I organized, edited, and printed much of his music, the results of which can now be found at the website www.leoornstein.net. Audio versions of many works can be found on YouTube.

The music in this volume has been chosen to demonstrate the diversity of styles in which Leo Ornstein wrote over the course of his lifetime. While some of his earlier works are more "radical" than some of the later ones, the notion that he moved from such early radicalism into neo-romanticism is belied by the contrast between the lyrical 4th Sonata (1918) and his final kaleidoscopic work, the 8th Sonata (1997). Throughout his life he comfortably spanned a diversity of idioms, often working simultaneously on pieces in completely different styles. In later life he sometimes combined divergent styles within a single work, as in his 3rd string quartet and his 8th Sonata. Through his entire life he resisted shoehorns of all sorts, always marching relentlessly to his own drummer.

SEVERO ORNSTEIN

Introduction

By 1912 Leo Ornstein was well on his way to establishing a major career as a virtuoso pianist. He had immigrated with his family to the United States from Russia in 1906, when he was twelve; graduated from the Institute for Musical Arts (later to become Juilliard); and he continued to study with the well-known pianist-pedagogue Bertha Feiring Tapper. He had begun to appear in public and had composed some, mostly conventional, parlor piano pieces. He had even made two recordings for Columbia, of music by Chopin and Grieg. The recordings, extant today, reveal a young artist whose virtuosity was already fully in bloom.

Then, as his concert career began to blossom, something happened. According to the composer, he began to hear strange musical sounds in his head—odd, dissonant chords. He played the chords on the piano, then started to expand on them. Soon he had written an entire piece based on those strange sounds, Funeral March of the Dwarfs, probably his first composition in this new, ultramodern style. Other pieces soon followed, especially what became his signature piece for a time, Danse Sauvage or Wild Men's Dance. Many years later Ornstein recalled his epiphany:

> Danse Sauvage was written by a young person with no experience whatever with modern music. I still wonder at the age of eighty, why should I have thought of that? A boy that had been sitting at the piano practicing the Twelfth Rhapsody to try to astonish the ladies with the speed and accuracy of the passages, and blind the audience with the terrific glissandos and what not. Why suddenly that thing came into my head—I'll be blessed if I know. And as a matter of fact, I really doubted my sanity at first. I simply said, what is that? It was so completely removed from any experience I had ever had.

He played it for Tapper, whose first reaction was to agree, he had lost his sanity. Later, many audiences felt the same, although possibly it is for that very reason that the piece generated an extraordinary level of excitement.

According to the composer, he had been studiously perfecting his traditional repertoire in the spring of 1913, and had no experience with ultramodern music when the new sounds suddenly appeared. We don't know what he encountered—he traveled to Europe in 1910 and in 1913, although whether Danse Sauvage was written before or after the second trip is unclear. Danse Sauvage does bear such resemblance to Ravel's Le Valse that for these two works to have been composed independently is a remarkable coincidence. Both have a driving triple rhythm, make use of edgy tone clusters, and are in a three-part ABA form.

Several other pieces in this ultramodern idiom soon followed, including Three Moods, Suicide in an Airplane, and Impressions of the Thames. By

1915, however, Ornstein had begun to rethink his direction: after composing his most radical, dissonant, unrelenting, atonal composition, the Sonata for Violin and Piano, Op. 31, Ornstein paused, realizing that he had taken his dissonant style as far as it could go: "I would say that Op. 31 had brought music just to the very edge.... I just simply drew back and said, 'beyond that lies complete chaos,'" and "after I have lain down on the piano keyboard and sounded all the notes at once—what then?"

It was this experimental music, however, that secured Ornstein's reputation. In early 1915 he gave a series of four concerts at the Bandbox Theatre in New York, at which he introduced America to a range of avant-garde music that was almost completely unknown in this country. It included newer works by European composers, Schoenberg, Ravel, Scriabin, Albéniz, as well as his own compositions. From then on Ornstein would be associated with musical radicalism, even though he performed a good deal of traditional music on the concert circuit.

Because of his compositions Ornstein became much more than just another Russian pianist. It is safe to say that between 1915 and 1920 he was the most notorious musician in America. By 1918, at age twenty-five, he had already become the subject of a full-length biography[1]. Chapters about him appeared in books by the critics Paul Rosenfeld and Carl Van Vechten; *The Musical Quarterly* and several literary magazines carried major essays[2]. Literally hundreds of newspaper articles discussed him. In 1916 Waldo Frank had prophesized that of Stravinsky, Schoenberg, and Ornstein, that "Ornstein, the youngest of these, gives promise to be the greatest." A year earlier, Herbert F. Peyser had observed that "the world has indeed moved between the epoch of Beethoven and of Leo Ornstein." That same year Charles Buchanan claimed that "potentially, he [Ornstein] is the most significant figure in today's music." Two years later the "potentially" was gone: Ornstein was "the most salient musical phenomenon of our time." James Hunecker, who found Ornstein the only "true-blue, genuine, futurist" composer alive, commented, "I never thought I should live to hear Arnold Schoenberg sound tame; yet tame he is, almost timid and halting

---

[1] Frederick Martens, *Leo Ornstein: The Man, His Ideas, His Work* (New York: Breitkopf & Härtel, 1918). Martens was known at the time for several books on music, most of them on opera, and for his operatic libretti and translations of libretti. He and Ornstein later collaborated on some songs, Martens providing the text.

[2] Paul Rosenfeld, *Musical Portraits: Interpretations of Twenty Modern American Composers* (New York: Harcourt, Brace and Company, 1920), 267–280; Carl Van Vechten, *Music and Bad Manners* (New York: Knopf, 1916), 229–43; Charles L. Buchanan, "Ornstein and Modern Music," *The Musical Quarterly 4,* no. 2 (April 1918), 174–83; Frederick Corder, "On the Cult of Wrong Notes," *The Musical Quarterly 1,* no. 3 (July 1915), 381–86; Margaret Anderson, "Leo Ornstein," *The Little Review 3,* no. 3 (May 1915), 13–15; Paul Rosenfeld, "Ornstein," *New Republic 7,* no. 82 (27 May 1916), 83–85. Lawrence Gilman discussed Ornstein at length twice in his column, "Drama and Music: Significant Happenings of the Month," *North American Review 201,* no. 713 (April 1915), 593–97, and *North American Review 203,* no. 722 (January 1916), 129–36.

after Ornstein." In London, an anonymous critic for the *London Observer,* dubbed Ornstein, "the sum of Schoenberg and Scriabin squared."[3]

Ornstein was well aware of the sensation he caused. Prior to his Bandbox concerts, he gave similar recitals in London, the first of which elicited the headline from *Daily Mail:* "Wild Outbreak at Steinway Hall." Ornstein later commented, "I couldn't hear the piano myself. The crowd whistled and howled and even threw handy missiles on the stage." He then smiled to the interviewer and commented, "But that concert made me famous."

Ornstein never abandoned dissonance and modernism, but he began to blend his radicalism with a more expressive, accessible style. He referred to his older, radical music as "experimental" and his newer style "expressive." Seven Fantasy Pieces, Impressions of Chinatown and the Piano Sonata No. 4, all written between 1915 and 1918, belong to the latter category. Yet, in spite of an apparent softening of dissonance, both his prior and post-1915 shorter piano pieces display a stylistic consistency. They are usually programmatic, they eschew counterpoint almost entirely, they are often in a more or less straightforward overall form such as ABA, they make considerable use of ostinato, and they often have a lyrical melodic line. Ornstein's greatest strength was as a lyrical melodist, even though his free use of chromaticism, dissonant harmony, and casual relationship with tonality sometimes masked that point.

Ornstein's programs might allude to a mood, a place, or an event. In many ways he was an impressionist, and he freely acknowledged a debt to Debussy. His programs grew from his own experience: Impressions of the Thames followed his 1913–14 trip to London, as Impressions of Chinatown did his visit to San Francisco. Newspaper accounts could also stimulate Ornstein's imagination, for example Suicide in an Airplane. In 1913 airplanes were barely beyond the Wright Brothers stage, and still in the hands of daredevils, experimentalists, and the armed forces. Air travel in the modern sense was still far in the future. On April 2, 1913, the *New York Times* ran an article with the headline, "Suicide in Aeroplane," about how a Russian army officer shut his engine off and fell six hundred feet to the ground. The event was so novel that suicide was not suspected until a note that the officer had left was found. On one level the piece describes the event itself, the buzz of the engine, and a sense of flight. More importantly Ornstein describes the inner turmoil of Lt. Perlovski, the Russian officer. His agitation grows

---

[3] Waldo Frank, typescript for an article "Leo Ornstein and the Emancipated Music," to appear in *The Onlooker* (1916), in Ornstein Collection, Yale Music Library, quoted in Vivian Perlis, "The Futurist Music of Leo Ornstein," *Notes 31,* no. 4 (June 1975), 741,. Charles L. Buchanan, "Futurist Music," *The Independent,* 31 July 1916, 160, "Ornstein and Modern Music," *The Musical Quarterly,* 4, no. 2 (April, 1918), 176. Herbert F. Peyser, "Inverted Philistinism of Futurism's Defenders," *Musical America,* 24, no. 24 (16 May, 1916), 22; James Huneker, *Columbus Sunday Dispatch,* 7 Jan. 1917, magazine section, p. 3,; James Grenville, "The Musical Futurist and His Sophisticated Discords," *NY Tribune,* 5 March 1916, p. 7. *London Observer,* quoted in Frederic Martens, *Leo Ornstein: The Man, His Ideas, His Work* (New York: Breitkopf & Hartel, 1918), 24–25.

gradually but inexorably, although the final catastrophic event is ignored under the imperative of ternary form, which demands a return to the beginning, and a gradual fade to a soft landing.

As reputation often determines perception, even though Chinatown or the Piano Sonata No. 4 does not have the harsh edge of Danse Sauvage or Suicide in an Airplane, audiences still considered Ornstein some kind of musical freak, and flocked to his concerts as if to witness a gladiator commit an act of musical mayhem. For whatever reason, Ornstein performances sold out, and between 1915 and 1925 he had a highly successful career as a concert artist. At that point, however, he made an extraordinary career choice. For a number of reasons Ornstein all but abandoned the concert stage to take up residence in Philadelphia, first as head of the Piano Department at the Philadelphia Music Academy, and then in 1934, to found, with his wife Pauline, the Ornstein School of Music. Although Ornstein had begun to withdraw from the concert world as early as 1922, to many his departure seemed precipitous and inexplicable. Leo Ornstein, one of the most well-known and successful artists in America, had disappeared from sight. Musical America lamented, in headlines, "Whatever Happened to Leo Ornstein?"

During his years in Philadelphia his compositional activity became more sporadic, until by the 1930s it had all but ended. Ornstein became a forgotten man. Then, in the 1970s, through a series of events, he was rediscovered. Concerts of his music were given, LP recordings were made, and he received the Marjorie Peabody Waite Award from the National Institute of Arts and Letters. The award was given every three years to a composer for significant lifetime achievement. This put Ornstein in league with Milton Babbitt, Leonard Bernstein, John Cage, Elliott Carter, Aaron Copland, Richard Rogers and others.

For Ornstein the immediate effect was to inspire him to start composing again. Most of the pieces in this volume that were not written in the 1910s are a direct result of the renewed interest in his music. He wrote many short works, some with obvious programmatic titles, such as A Long Remembered Sorrow, or A Morning in the Woods, some with more generic musical titles, such as waltz, impromptu, or fantasy piece. They continue much in his post-1915 style, only with different emphases. His driving dissonance has given way to a more introspective poetic style, allowing his lyricism to come more to the fore. The melodies are often elaborate filigrees, and entire pieces reflect Ornstein's easy virtuosity. A Morning in the Woods typifies his later short compositional style, although, probably in order to maintain the impressionistic mood, it is quieter and more delicate than some of his other works, in which the virtuosity is more apparent.

Ornstein's title Metaphor deserves special comment. He composed sixteen such works, which are undated but probably written in the 1960s and 70s. They are abstract, giving no suggestion as to their allusional content. In the 1990s Ornstein's son Severo collected them, and Ornstein stated at that time they should be entitled metaphors. In a letter to Severo, Ornstein observed, "As in all the arts the implication can sometimes be greater than the reality," and instructed Severo to "put this on as motto in front of the metaphors. Ornstein, obviously pleased with this thought, added, "P.S. May I say myself that I've made up a pretty good aphorism."

Ornstein was an intuitive composer. He heard music in his head, and for him composing was a way to exorcise those sounds. Often he would hear a piece in its entirety; at other times he would improvise around the sounds he heard until the shape he wanted emerged. Charles Buchanan, who knew Ornstein in the 1910s, observed that Ornstein claimed he was "a kind of passive transmitter" through which his pieces come to the world, and that his music is "an unpremeditated music, a sort of spontaneous combustion." His shorter pieces seem to fit that description, emerging suddenly, whole. His larger works, however, required planning, development, and experimenting, in other words, working out the problems of large-scale forms.

Ornstein never studied composition, either at the Petrograd Conservatory or the Institute of Musical Arts. His innate musical abilities were so strong that he saw no need for theory or counterpoint courses, and was at best a recalcitrant student in those classes. Later he would have to struggle with some compositional issues, and that struggle is apparent in the Fourth Sonata as well as some other earlier multi-movement compositions. By the time he wrote his last two piano sonatas, the Seventh and Eighth, however, he had largely come to terms with this limitation. These two works, it should be noted, were composed when he was ninety-five and ninety-seven years old.

Piano Sonata No. 4, written in 1918, shows the pianist-composer in high virtuosic form. We hear echoes of Ornstein's signature Wild Men's Dance in the background of this rhapsodic work along with Borodin's Polovetsian Dances, whose melodies are never far from the surface, but then neither is Debussy's Claire de Lune. Brahms makes an appearance as duplets tug against triplets and inner lines sing alto melodies. Voices from the whole of the turn-of-the-century musical world are audible in the opening minutes of the work and throughout the sonata. In true Ornstein fashion, melodic fragments circle and swirl resisting the urge to settle.

Ornstein rushes into the first movement with a forte flourish the likes of which are normally reserved for later moments in a movement. Listeners are dropped into what sounds like the middle of the work. Incessant left-hand arpeggiated figures support a sinuous melody and motor toward a dolce passage where the music temporarily calms down, but the respite in action is short-lived. For the remainder of the movement, agitato and appassionato passages trade center stage before relinquishing their place to a tranquillo close.

The Semplice second movement begins more traditionally, but adds yet another voice to the chorus of musical influences when Ornstein channels Satie's soft-spoken, transparent, slightly exotic soundworld. Lopsided triple rhythms reminiscent of the French master's Gymnopédies hold until a con fuoco passage introduces a passionate interruption. Here the triple meter gives way to a spirited 6/8 passage, which melds into a Largamente that vacillates between bold statements in five and two and four beats. Ornstein rounds out the movement with a return to the opening thematic material that now expands to include a throaty melodic statement in an inner voice. Arpeggiated flourishes evocative of the opening of the first movement close the second one.

Ornstein joins the pianissimo close of the second movement to an equally quiet, but additionally melancholy Lento third movement. While filigree-like figures continue to decorate the musical fabric, there is an introspective, more direct, blues-like feel to this third part of the sonata. Momentum that had built up over the first two movements dissipates in a gently rocking 4/4 that holds until the close is imminent. Five measures from the end Ornstein seemingly slows down the tempo by adding fifth and sixth beats; the music exhausts itself as it wafts towards the highest reaches of the keyboard triple piano.

The work closes with a highly charged rhythmic vivo as Ornstein reclaims his assertive self. The movement starts forte and gets louder; it ultimately finishes tempestoso ed appassionato and triple forte. A prominent theme rides on top of a series of stacked thirds; it recalls the serpentine melodic material first heard in the opening movement, and it will inform all aspects of this final one. As in Wild Men's Dance, Ornstein wrings his fragmentary tunes dry. He moves them to different registers; he clothes them in new harmonic dress; he throttles up their dynamic level; he shifts their rhythmic framing. As with the earlier work, Piano Sonata No. 4 consumes itself in a barbarous display of pianistic fireworks. In 1918, despite his move to a more expressive style, Ornstein's personal Wild Man still lives.

Piano Sonata No. 8 was Ornstein's last major work and is one of his best compositions. As such it forms a fitting culmination to a compositional career that spanned almost ninety years. The first movement, entitled "Life's Turmoil and a Few Bits of Satire," is big, powerful, opening with a dramatic, unison theme. There are frequent tempo and mood changes, characteristic of Ornstein's larger works, but the entirety is integrated in a way that sometimes eluded Ornstein. Most of the movement vacillates between "turmoil" and a quality of melancholic nostalgia. Satire enters later, in a presto section Ornstein labels "Burlesca," which captures the mood in a rapid, jaunty duple meter. Lest there be any doubt about his intention he instructs the pianist on the next page, "Keep hammering away—this is obviously a take-off."

The middle movement, "A Trip to the Attic—a Tear or Two for a Childhood Forever Gone," consists of four short, simple, independent units: "The Bugler," "A Lament for a Lost Toy," "A Half Mutilated Cradle—Berceuse," and "First Carousel Ride and Sounds of a Hurdy Gurdy." The movement as a whole forms a striking contrast to the more expansive virtuosity of the rest of the work. Ornstein himself observed, "Some may object to the middle four Vignettes as an intrusion; others may find them a distinct contrast and relief from the brusqueness of the rest of the sonata." The Vignettes also suggest that even in his winter years Ornstein remained haunted by his childhood, by the pain felt from the removal from his home in Kremenchug and his placement in the Conservatory in St. Petersburg when he was ten years old, and the subsequent sudden departure from Russia to America two years later.

The Third movement has a more general title, "Disciplines and Improvisations." While it would be folly to divide the parts by the programmatic suggestions, the title in one sense is a metaphor of Ornstein's compositional approach, principally improvisational, but with a hard-earned discipline he had to acquire as he moved from short character pieces to the larger forms. Ornstein's mood changes are inevitably there, but overall the movement is a presto romp to a big closing climax, confirmed by the Ivesian instruction, "Give it all you've got to the very end." That seems an appropriate epithet for Ornstein. He continued to compose into his 101st year, but there were no more major pieces after this one.

MICHAEL BROYLES AND DENISE VON GLAHN

Suicide in an Airplane

Leo Ornstein

Allegro Molto

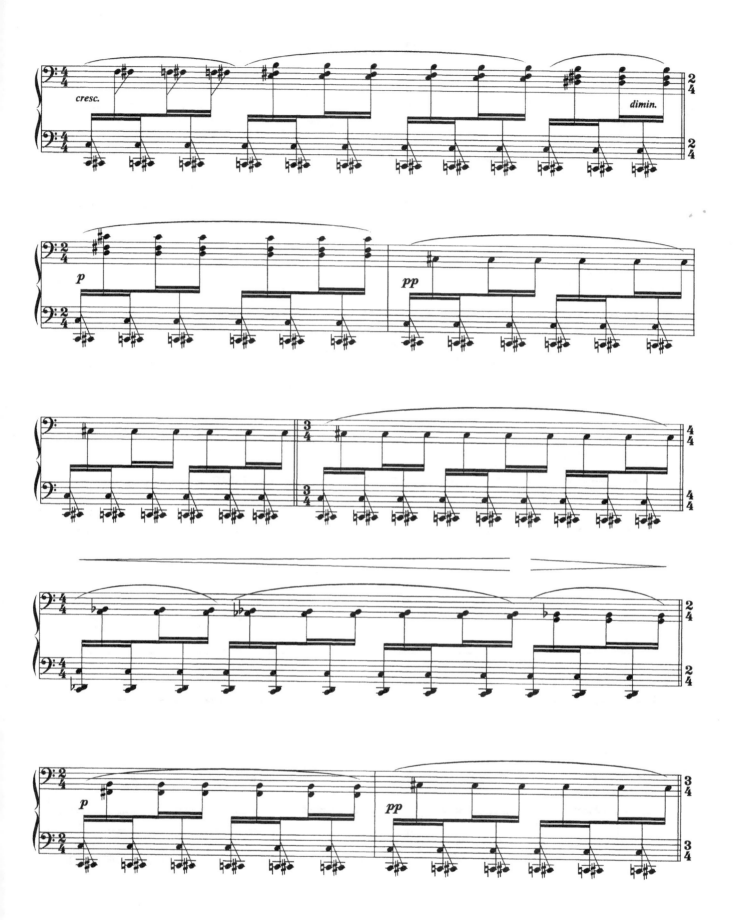

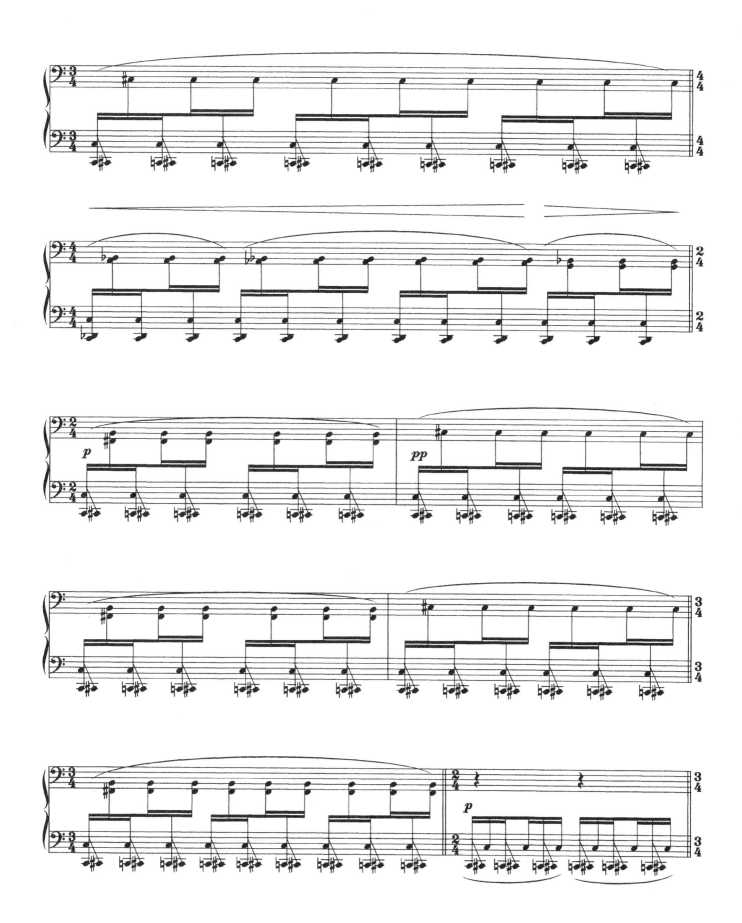

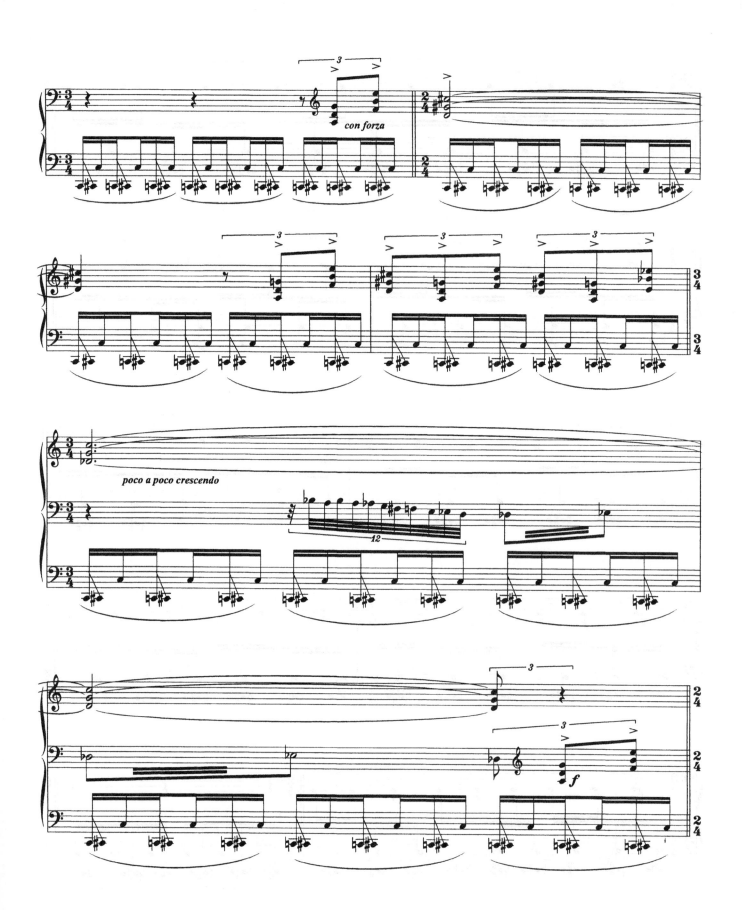

4

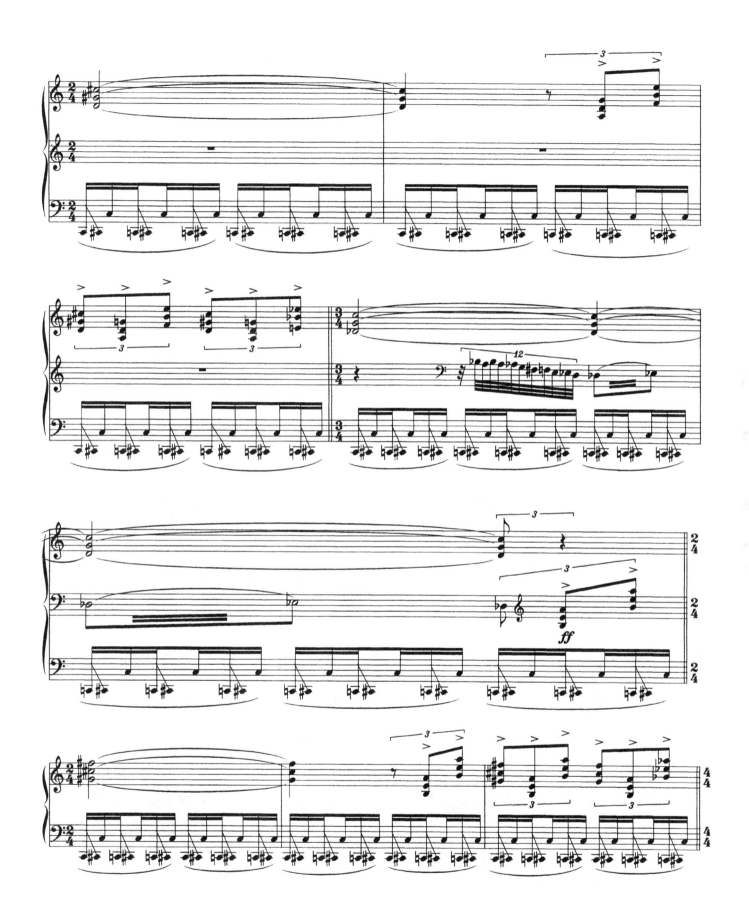

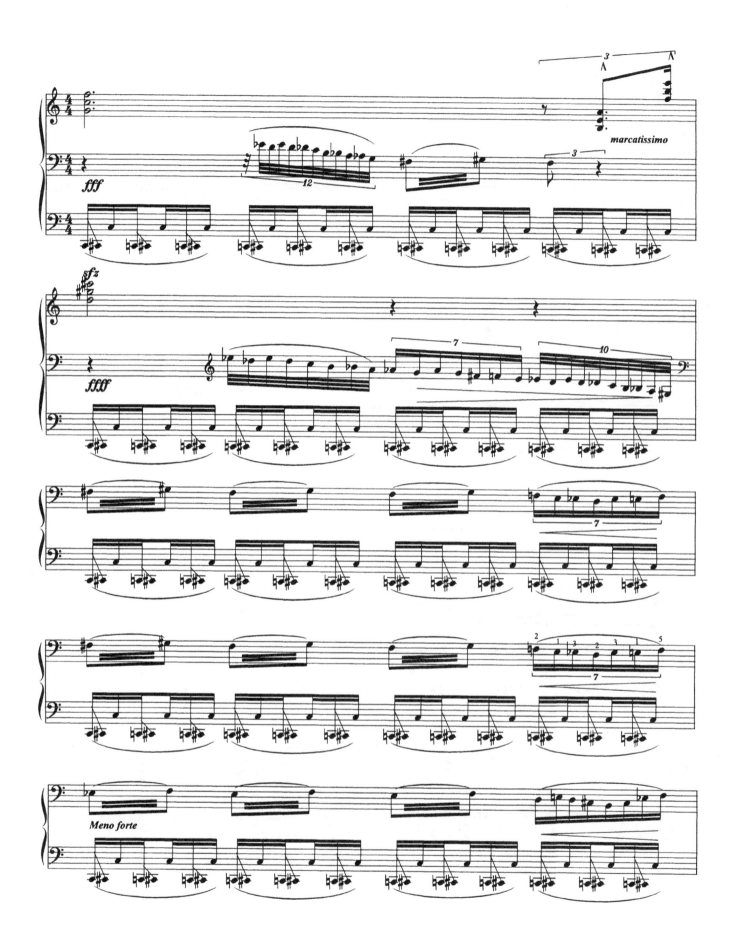

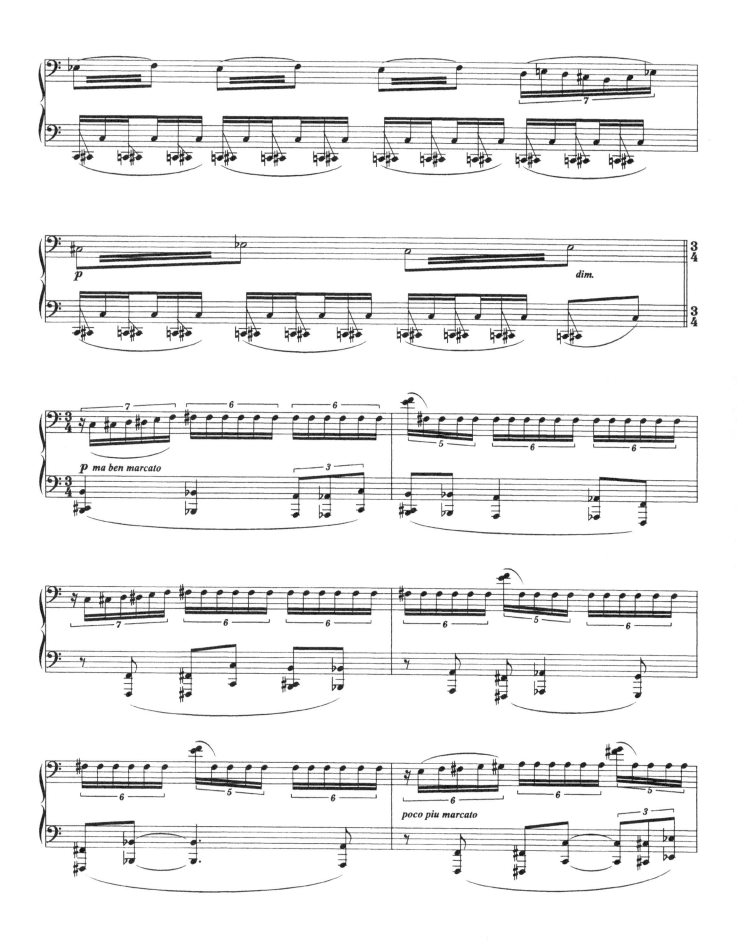

Poco piu mosso

poco a poco agitato e cresc.

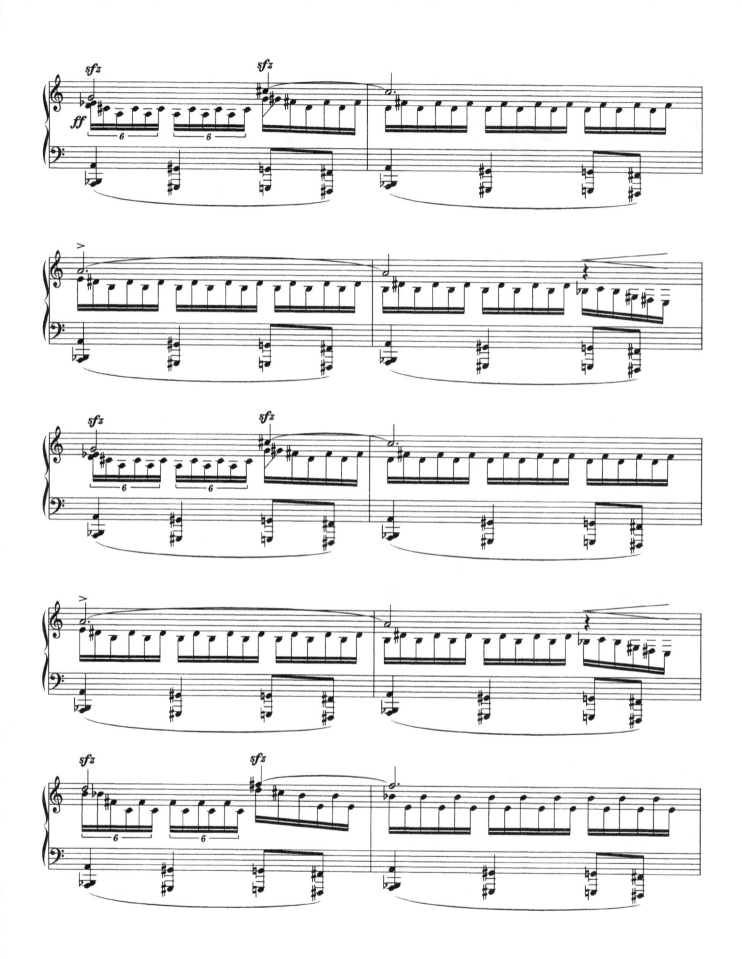

Tempo Imo

13

Three Moods

Anger

Throughout all three Moods accidentals apply only to those notes before which they stand. They do not carry through the measure.

16

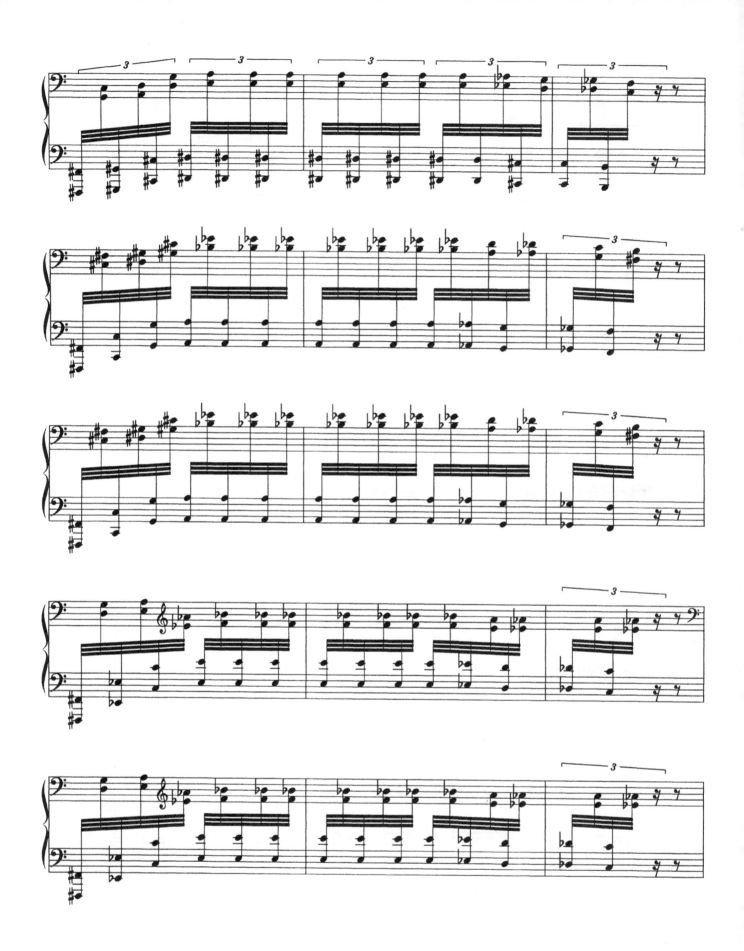

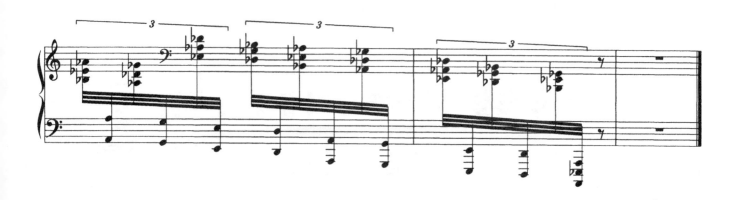

Grief

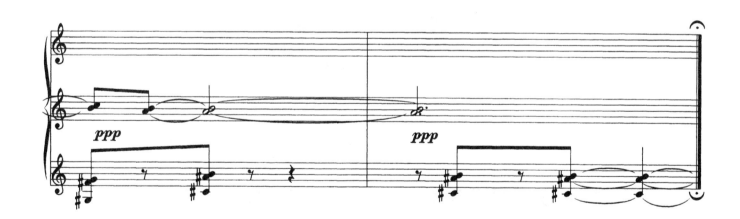

Joy

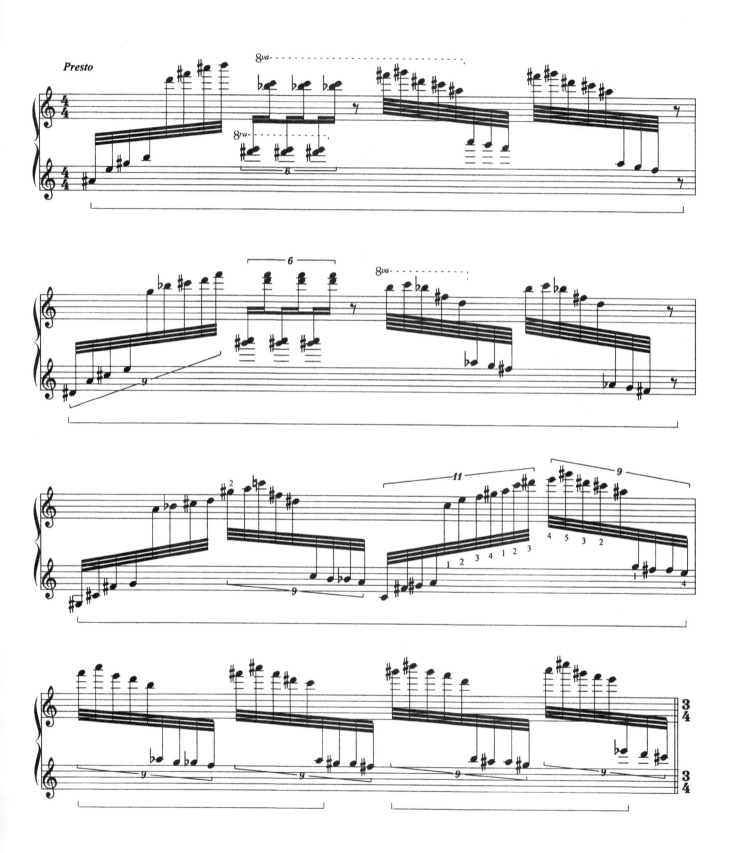

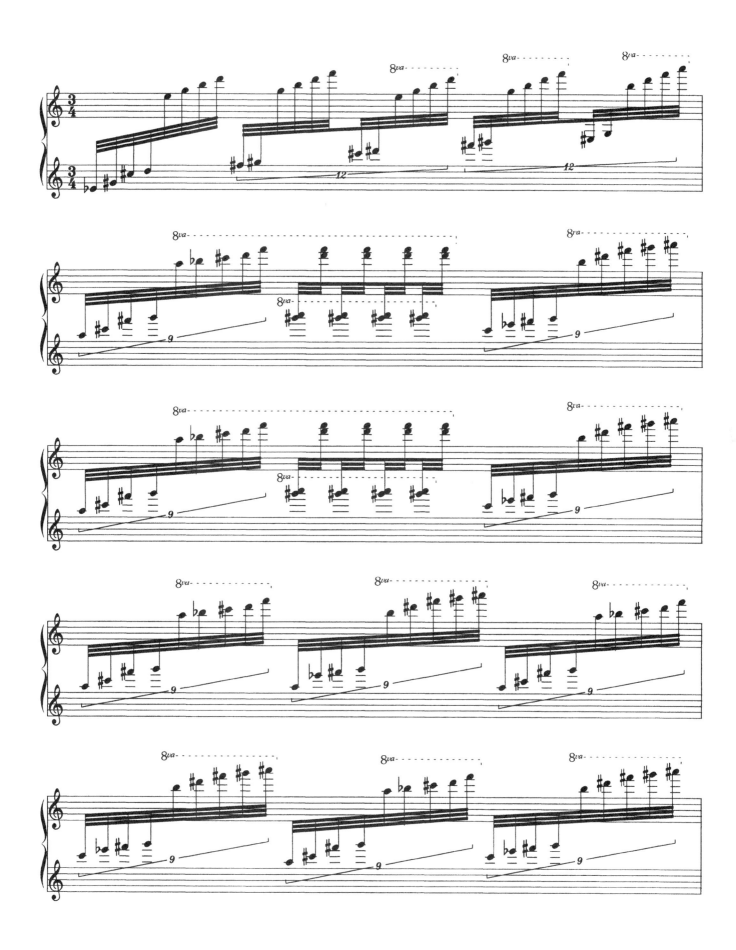

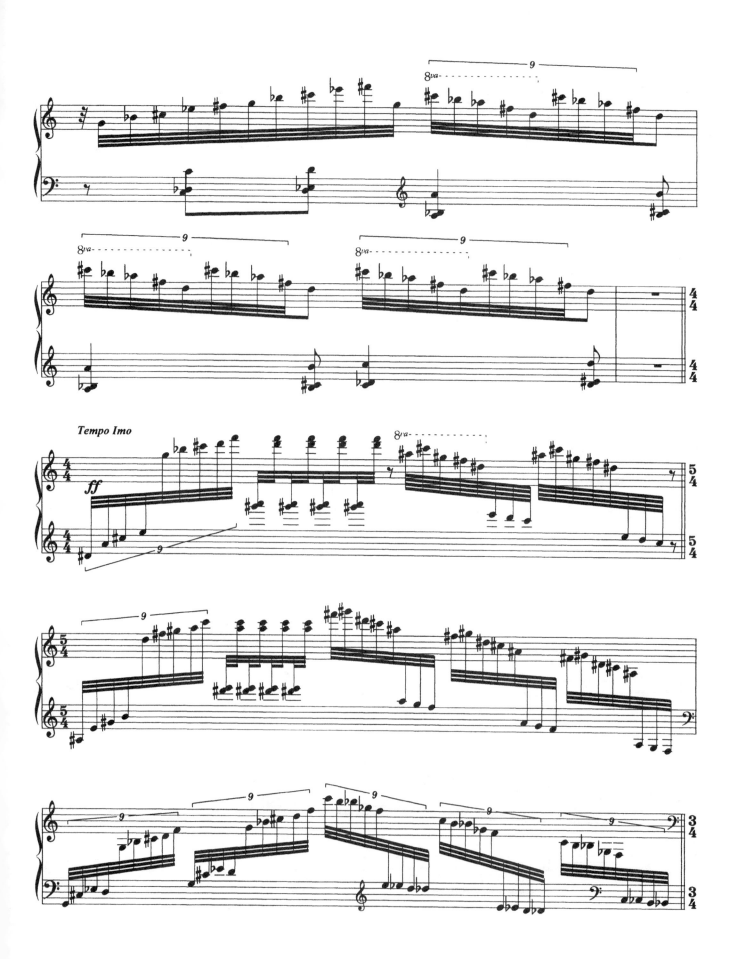

poco a poco f ed agitato

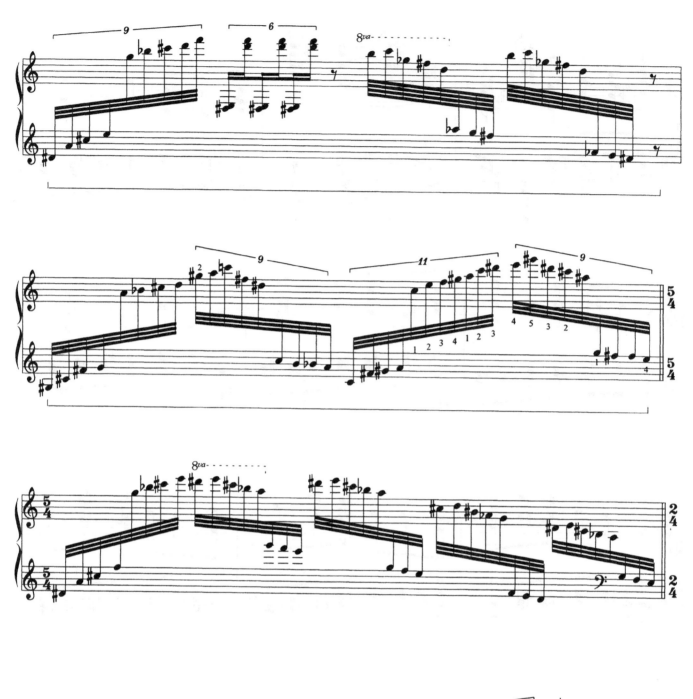

Wild Men's Dance

To my dear "MUMS".

Leo Ornstein

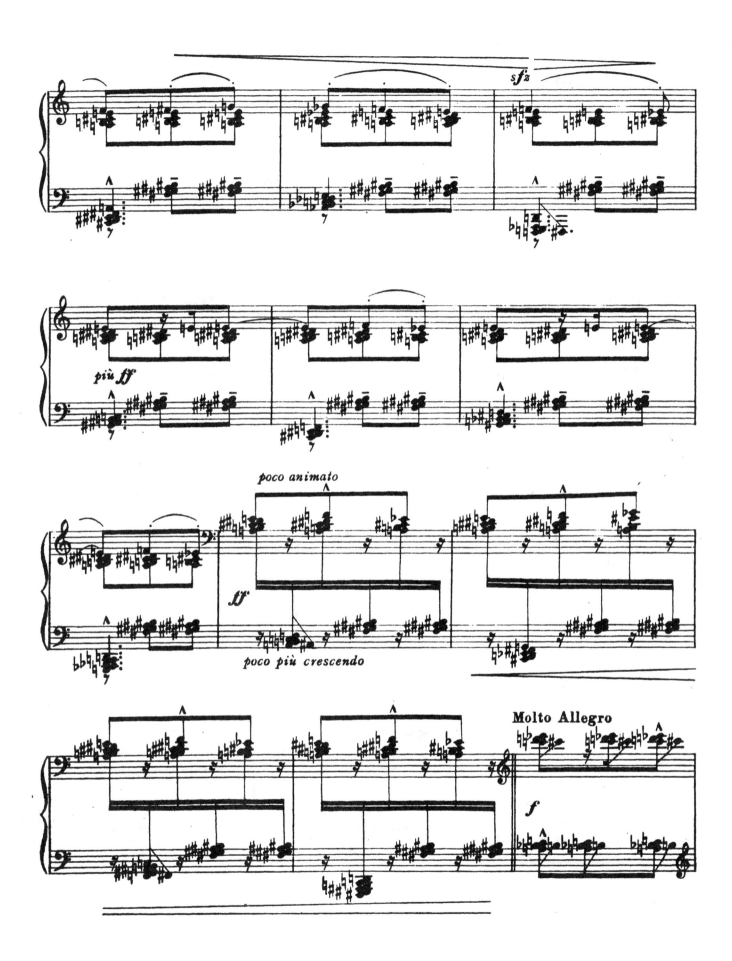

46

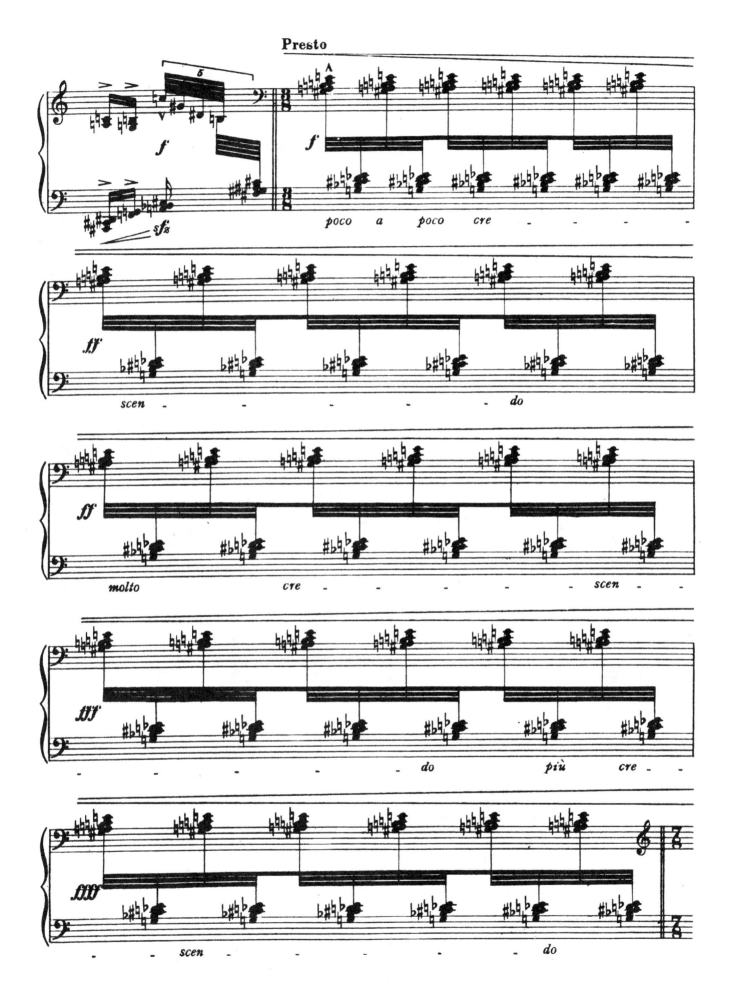

Presto

poco   a   poco   cre - - - -

scen - - - - - do

molto   cre - - - - scen - -

-   -   -   -   - do   più   cre - -

-   - scen - - - - - do

49

Vivo

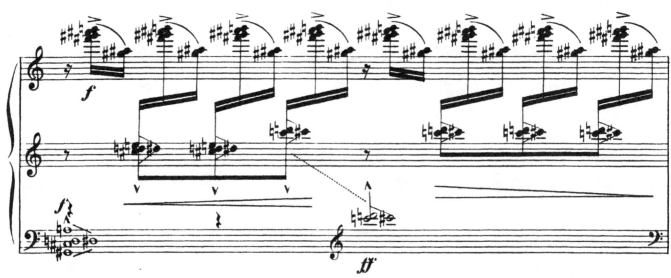

Poco a poco Presto

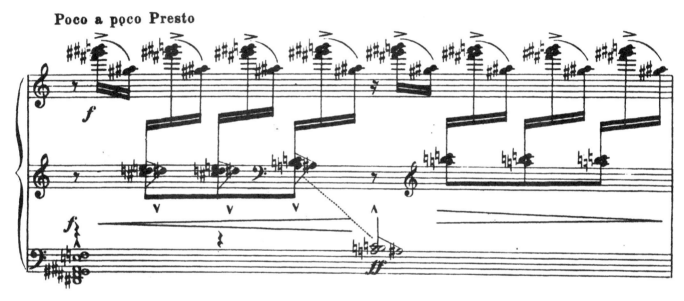

Più presto

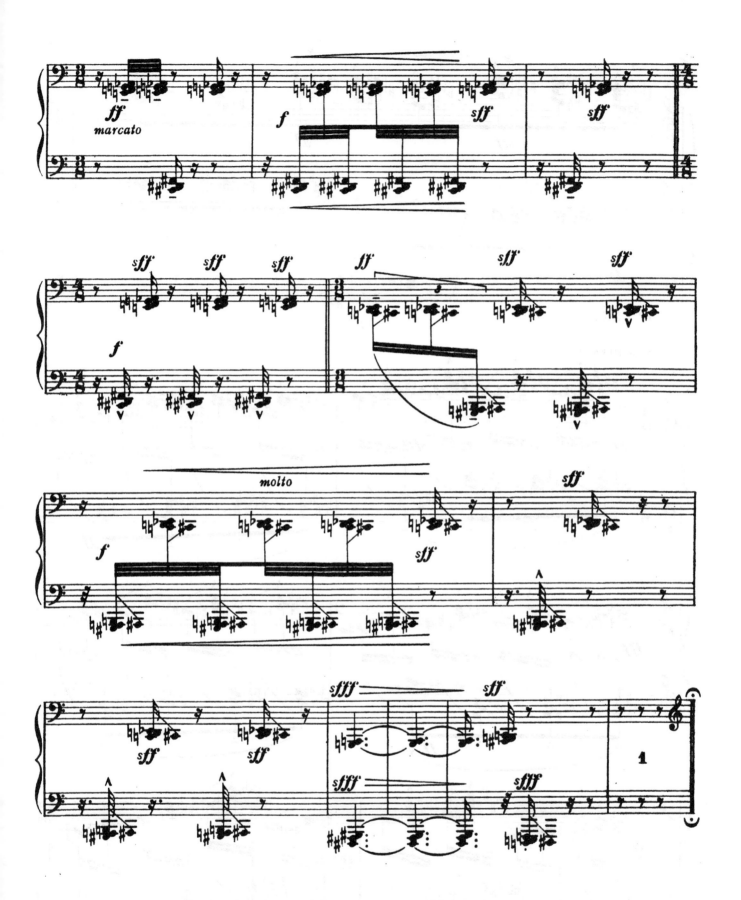

Tempo I

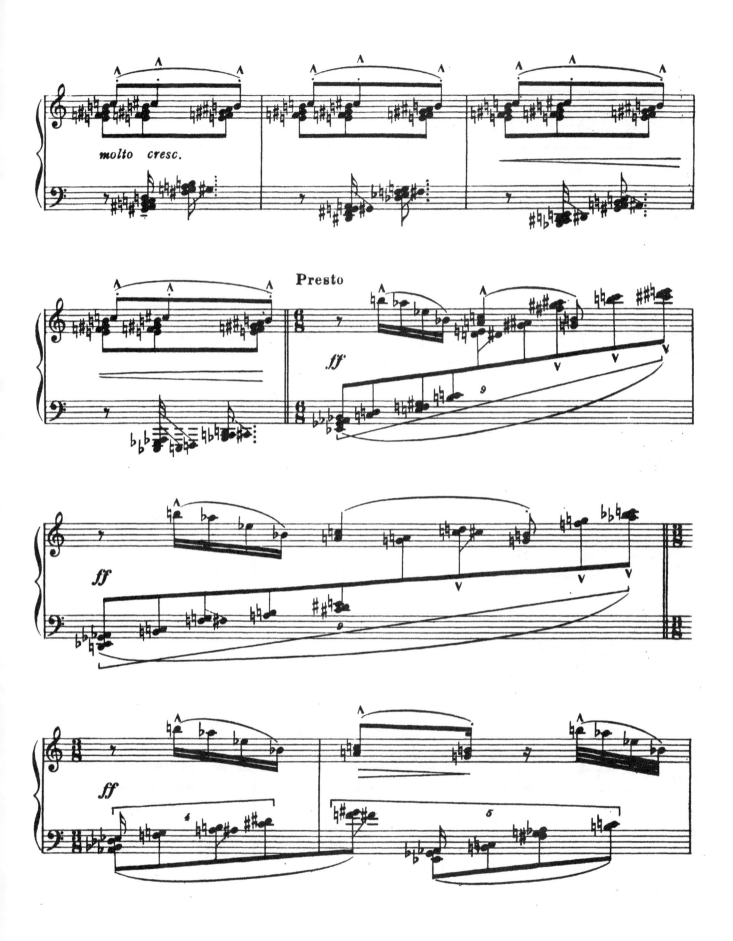

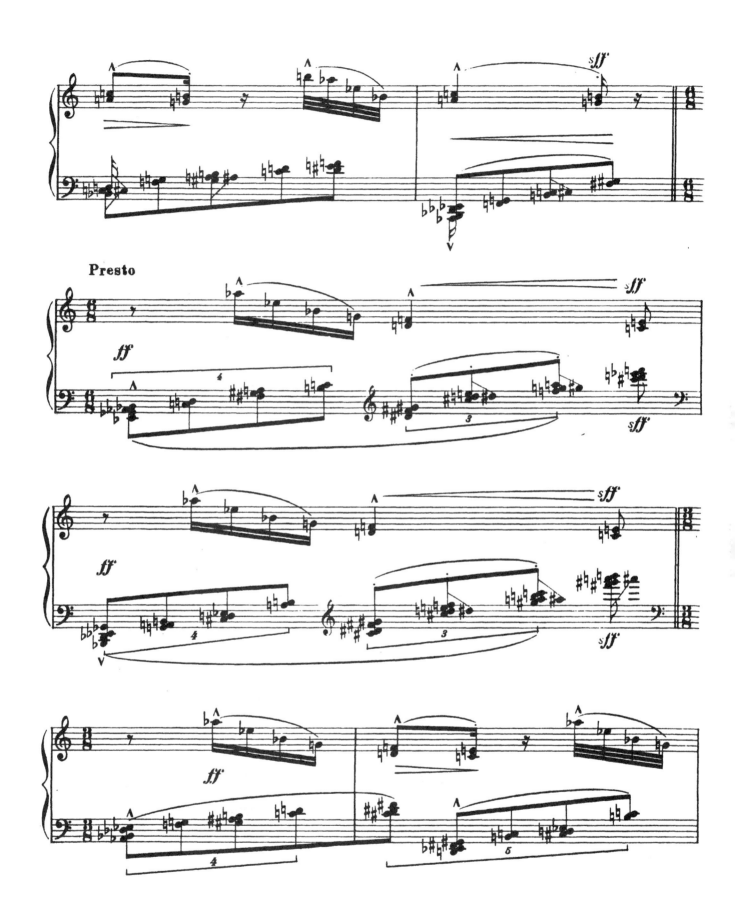

Presto

To Mr. Rudolf Ganz

Impressions of Chinatown

Leo Ornstein

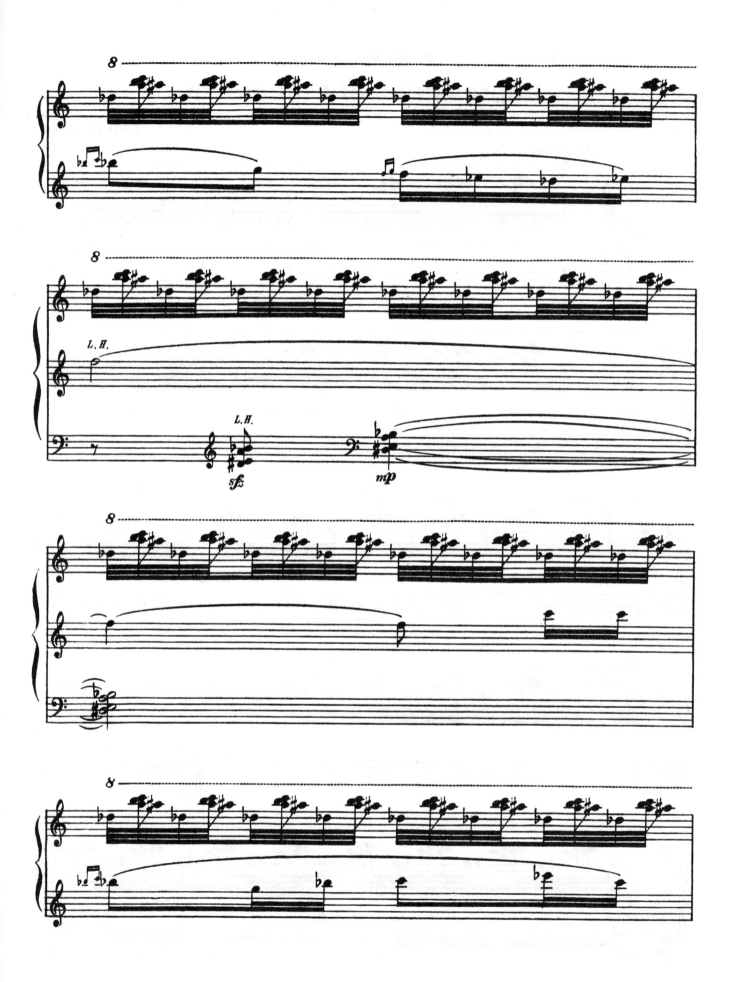

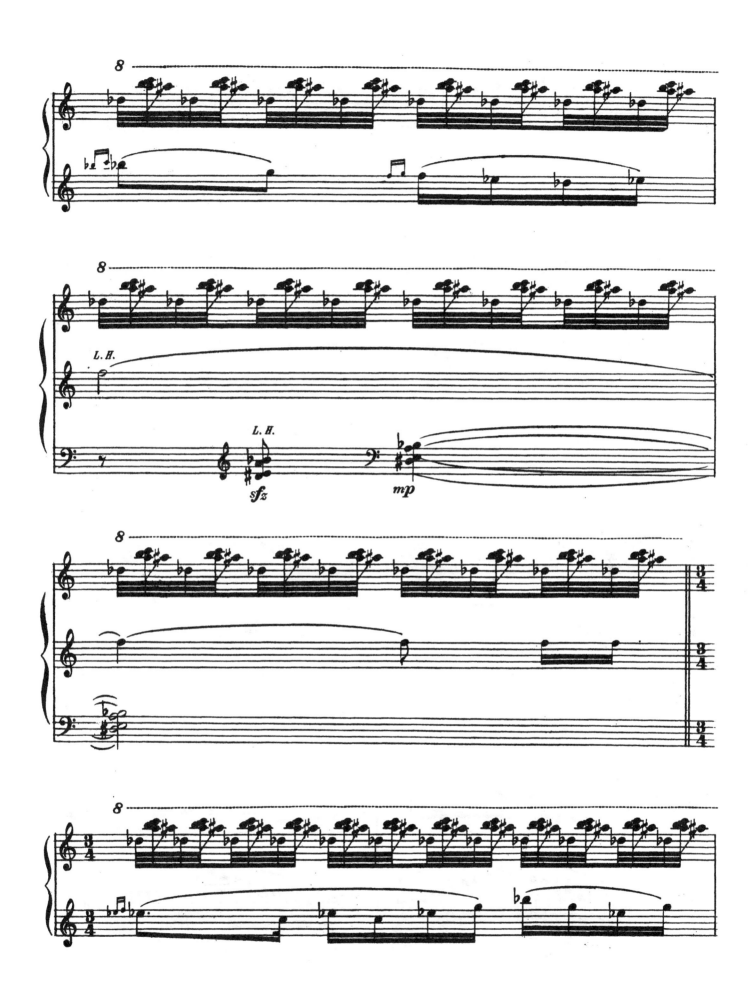

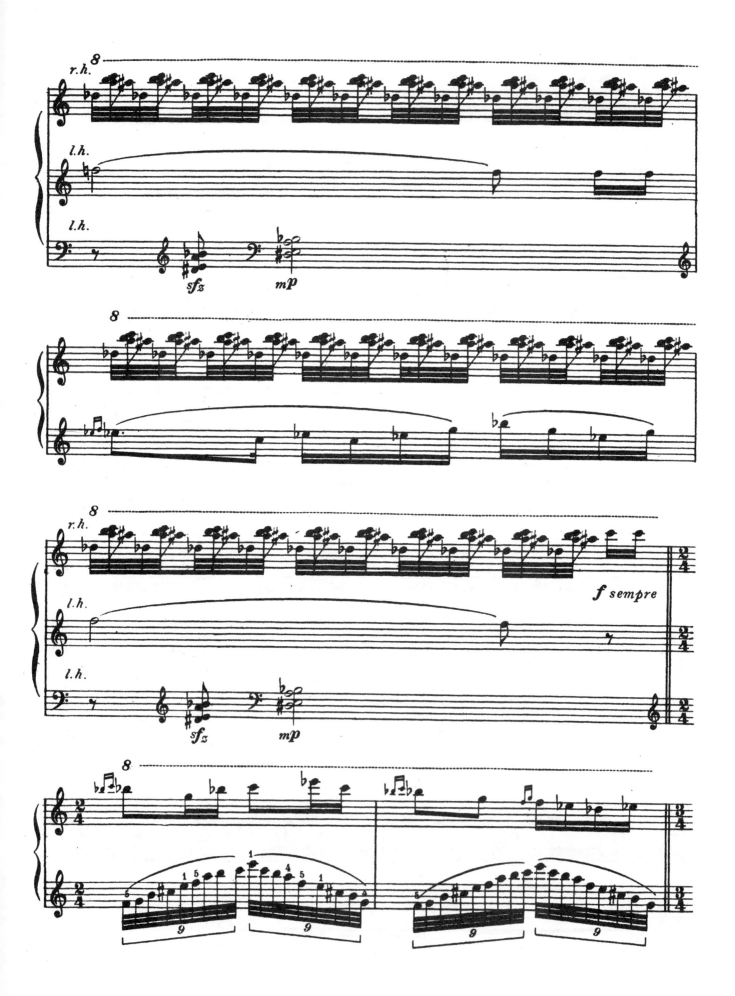

66

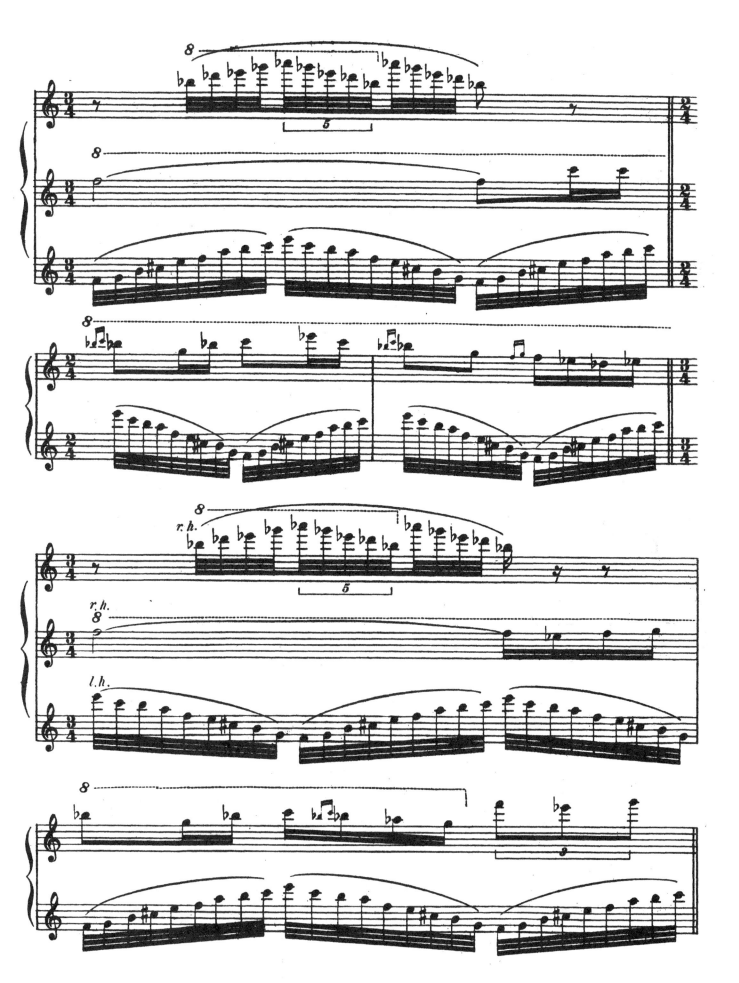

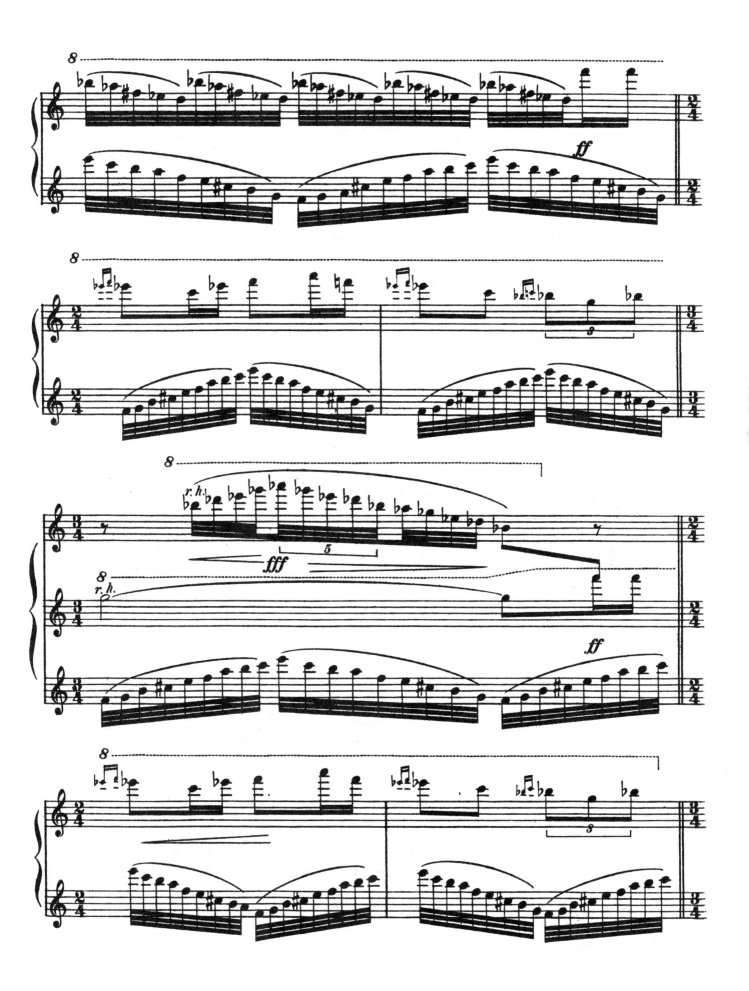

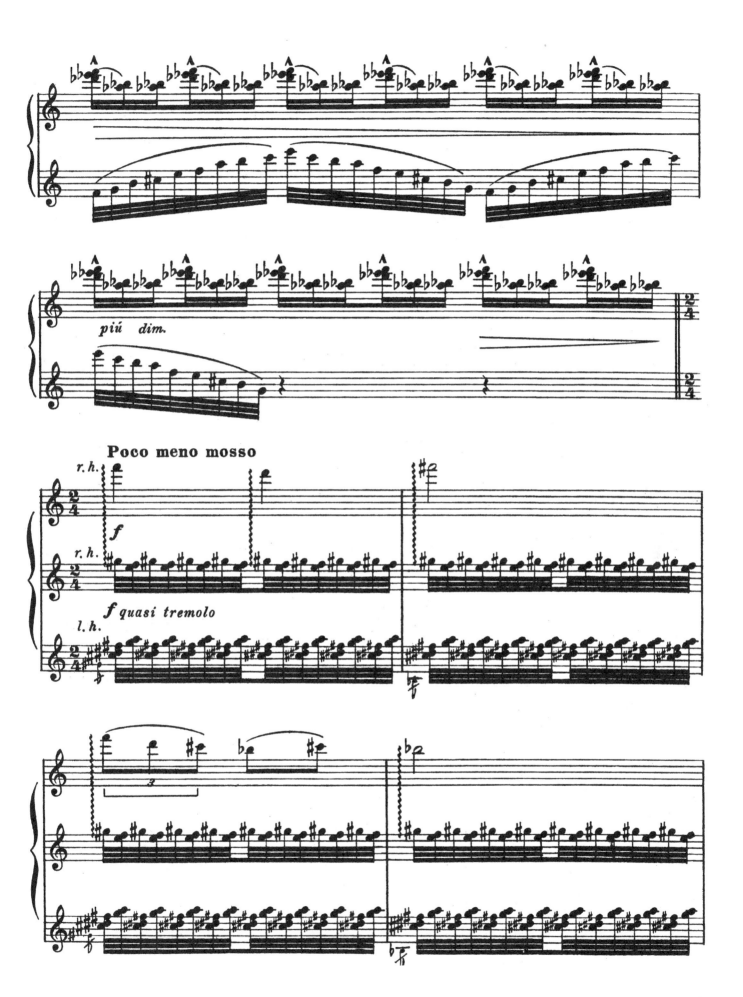

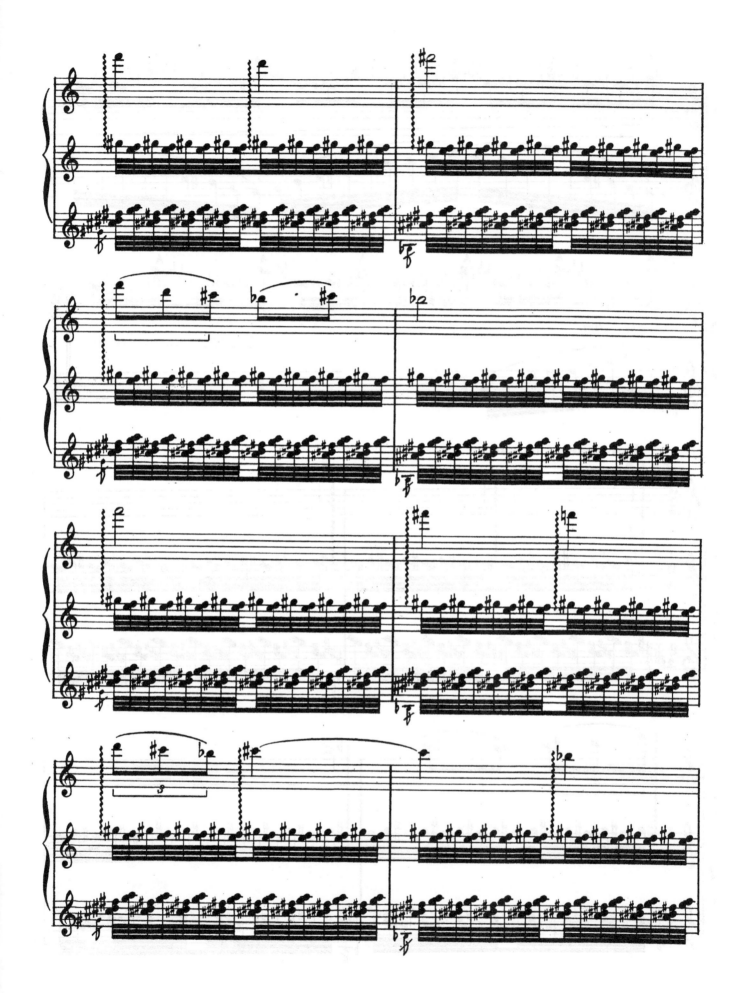

73

75

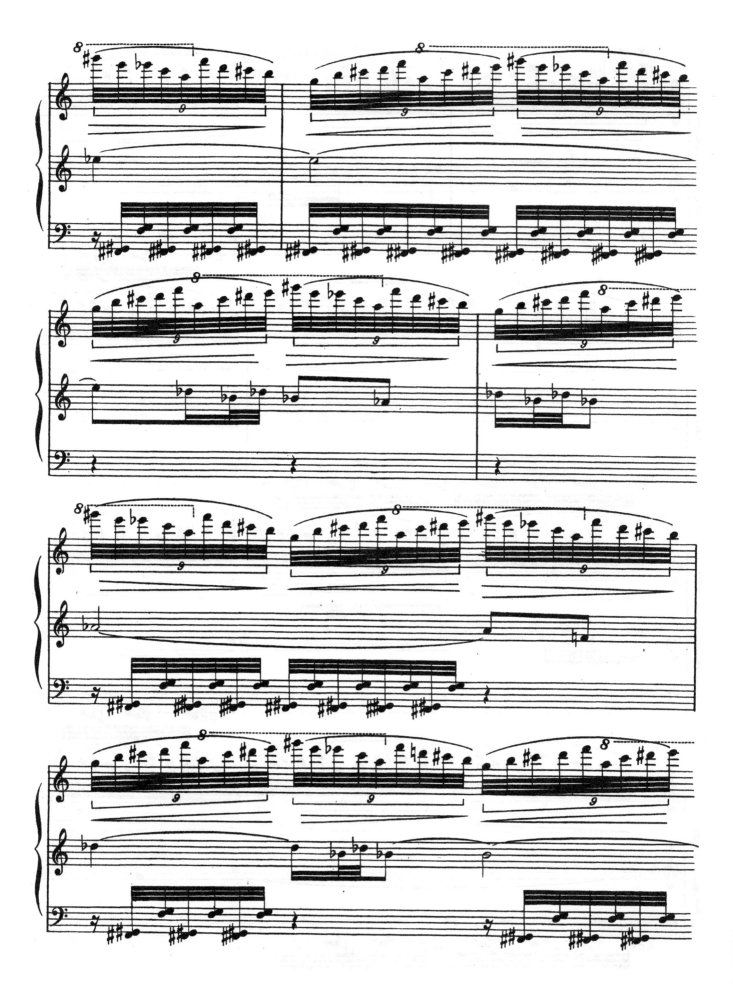

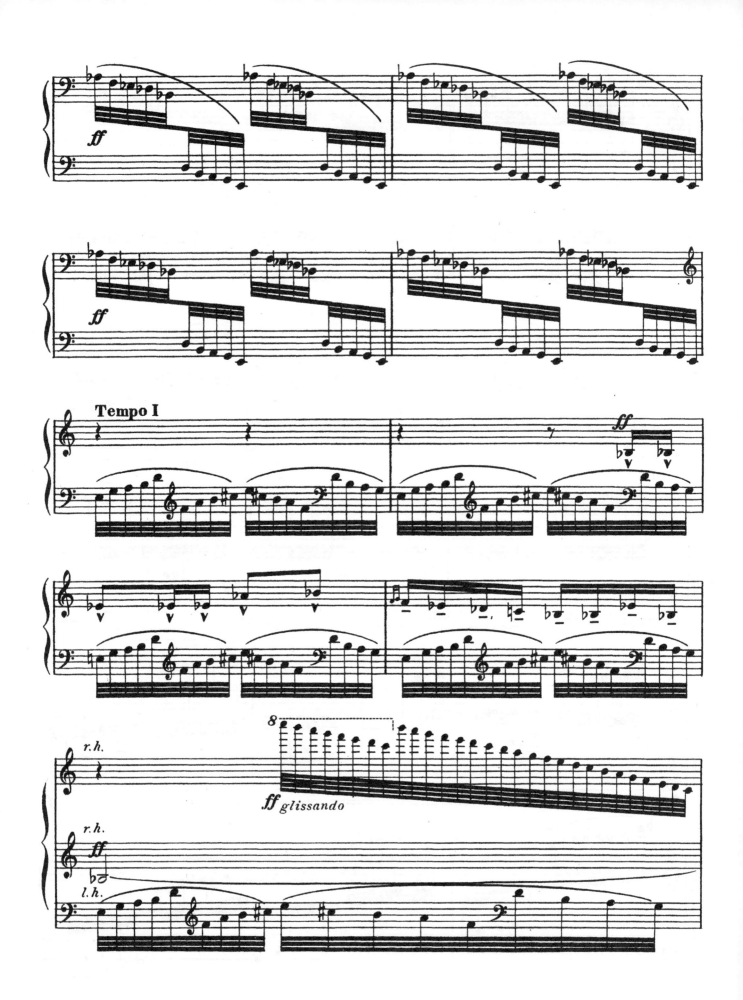

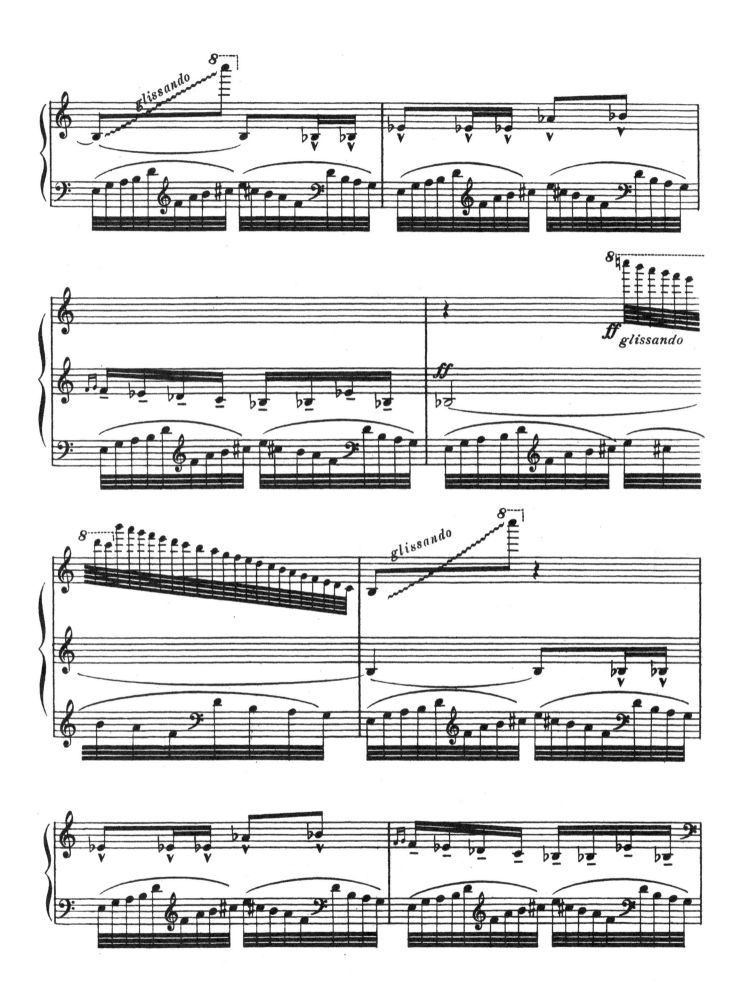

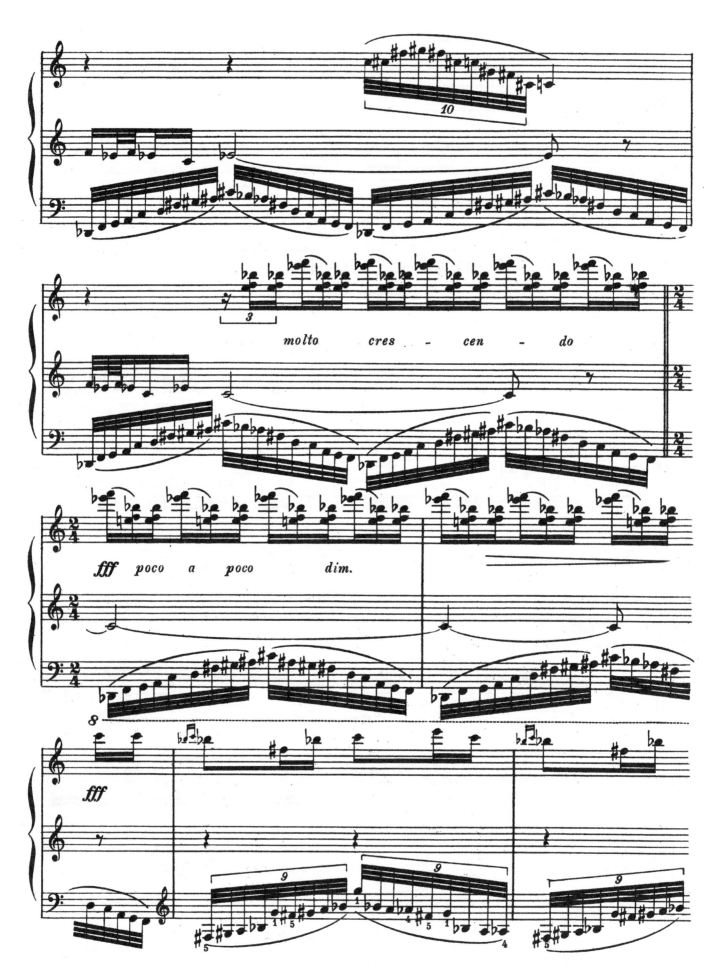

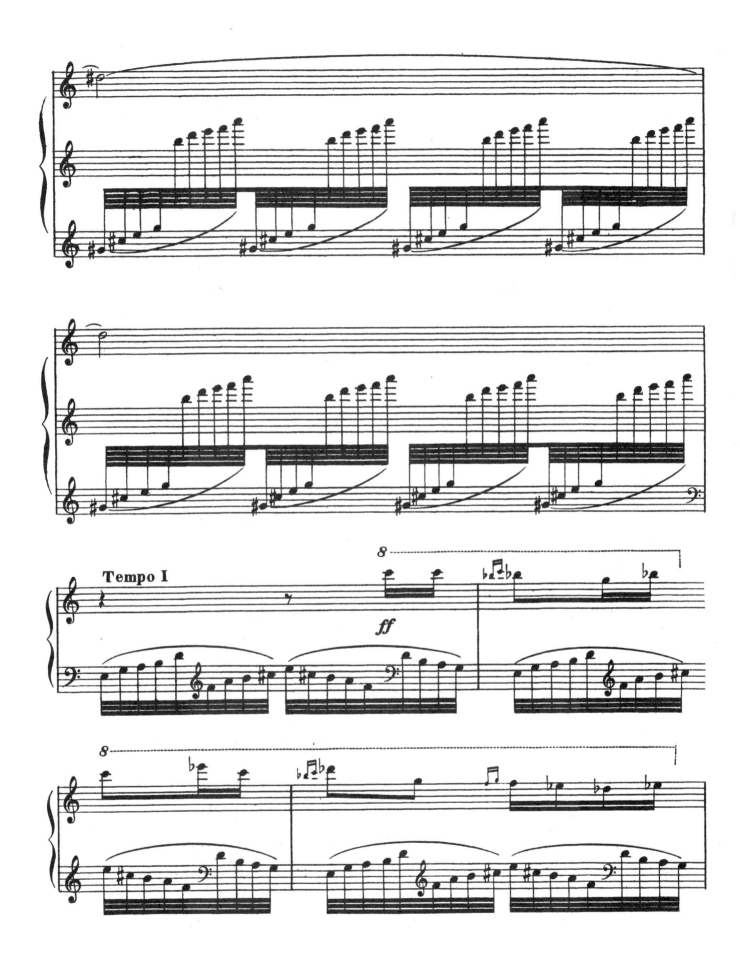

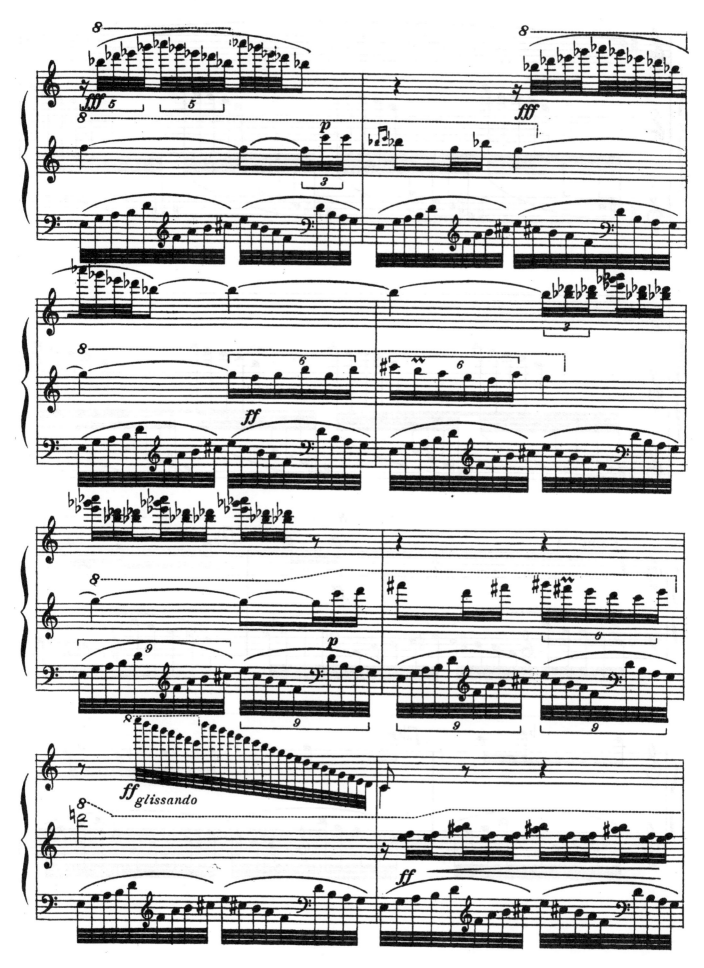

Piano Sonata No. 4

I

Leo Ornstein

Moderato assai

Tempo I°

100

II

104

III

111

IV

Furioso

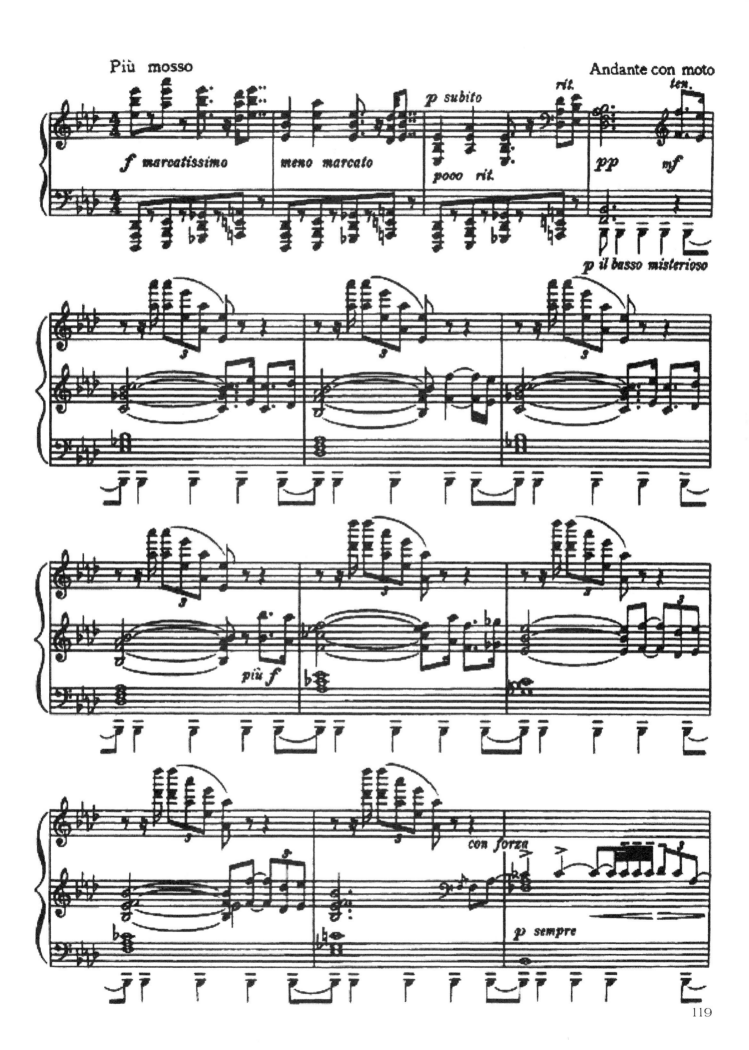

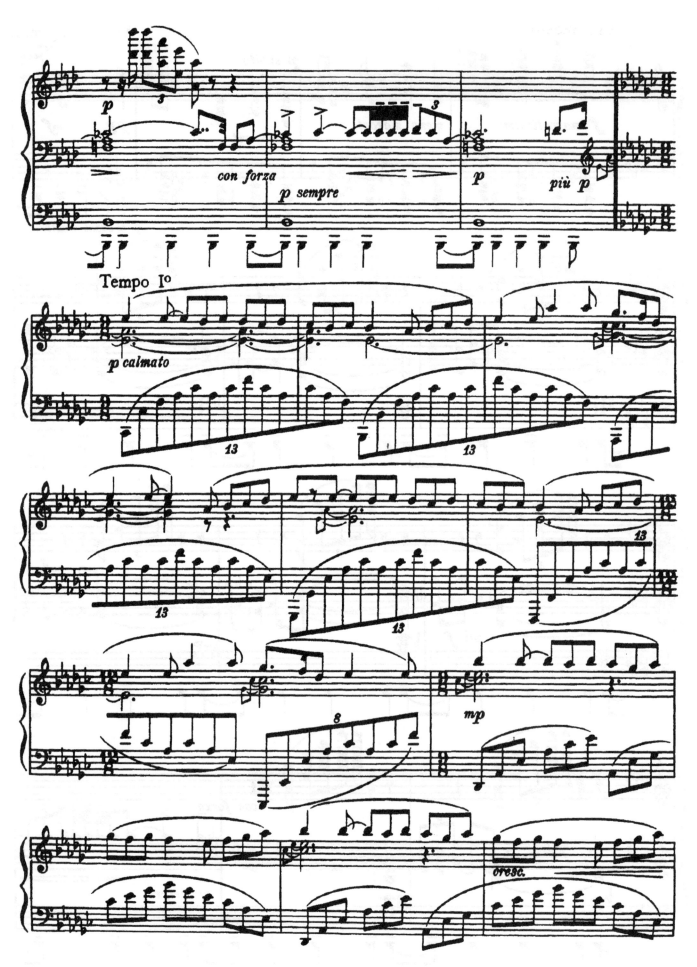

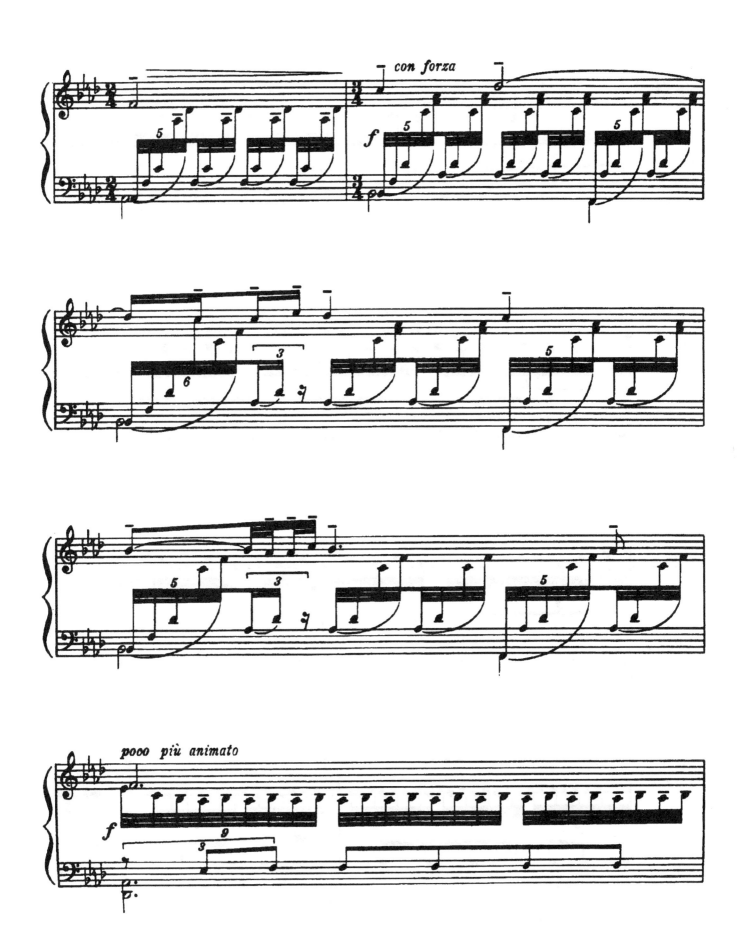

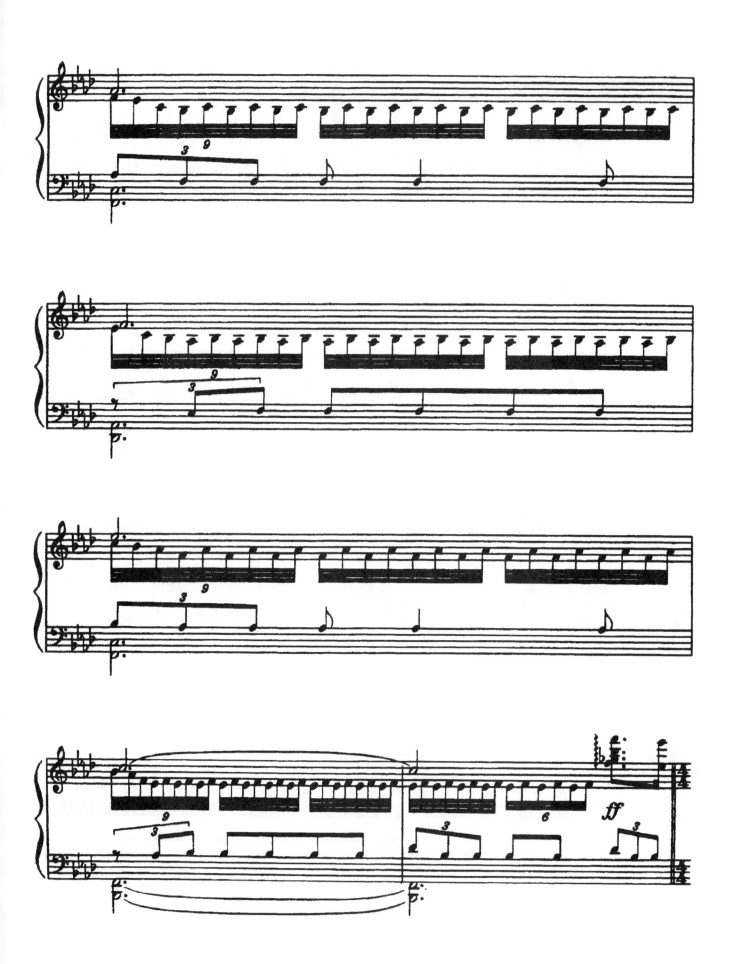

127

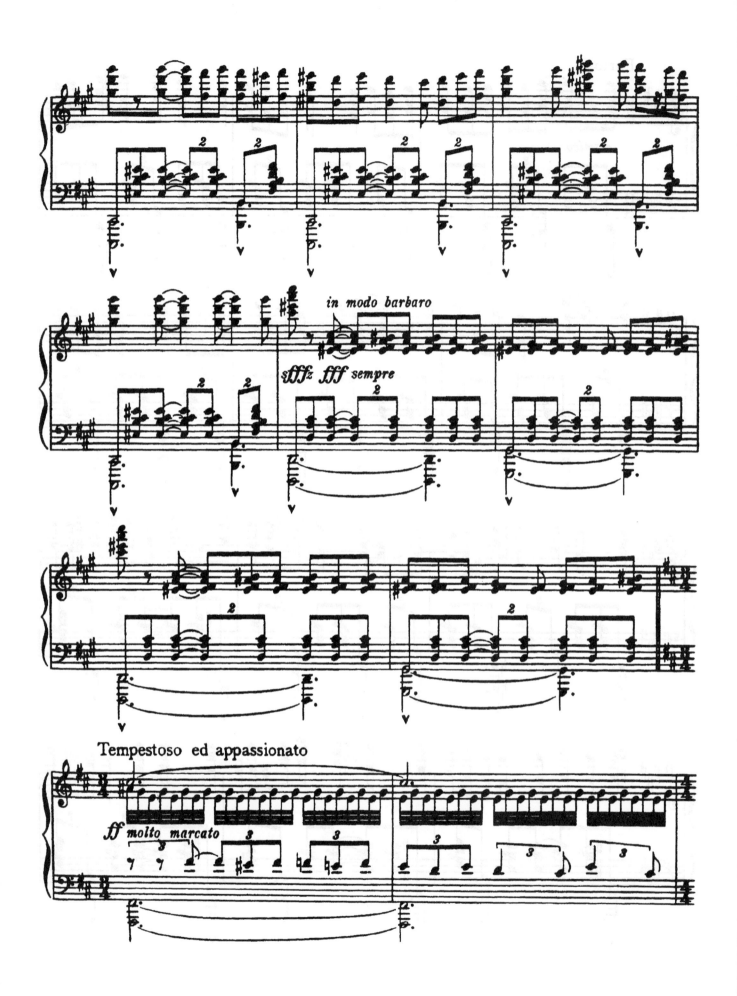

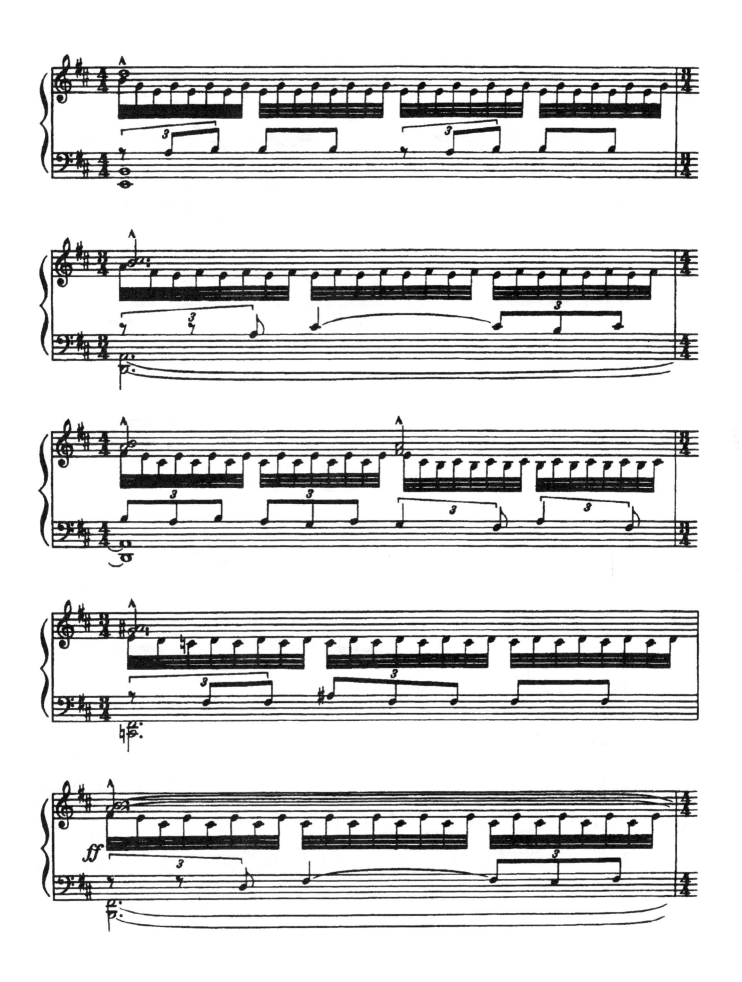

à M. D. Calvocoressi

Impressions of the Thames

Leo Ornstein

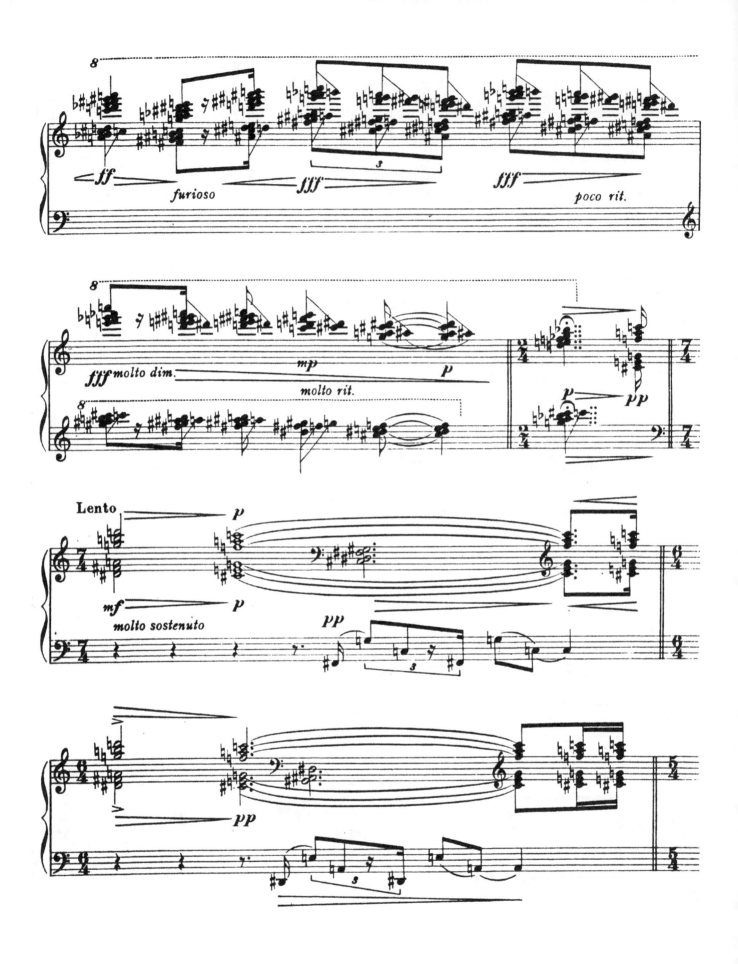

143

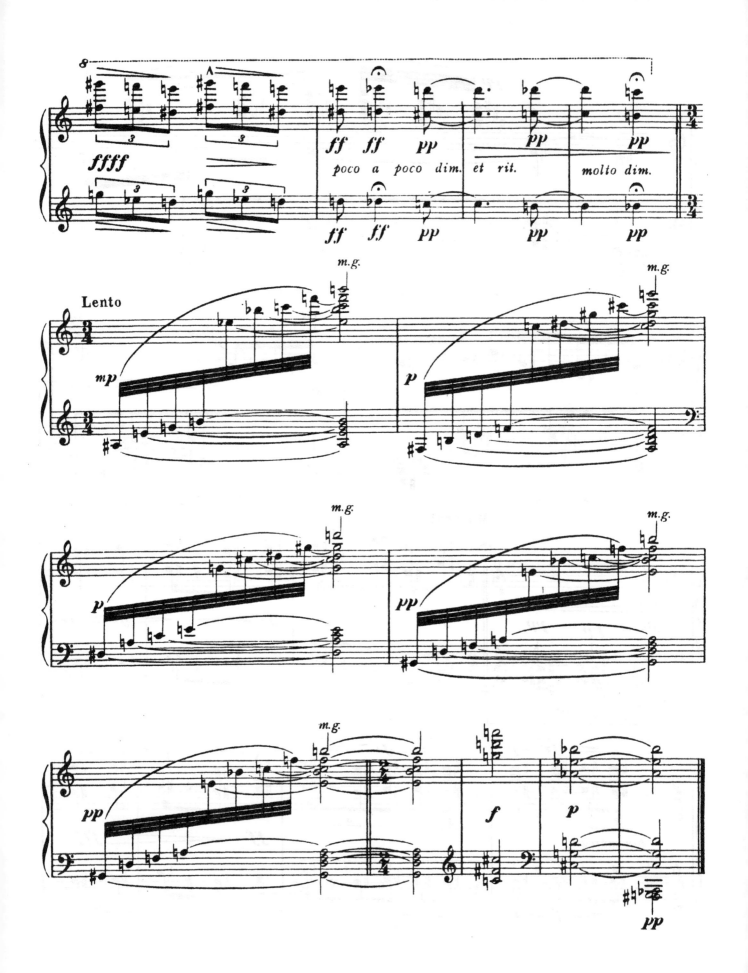

Impromptu No. 1

Leo Ornstein

Fantasy Piece No. 3

Leo Ornstein

162

163

Tarantelle

Leo Ornstein

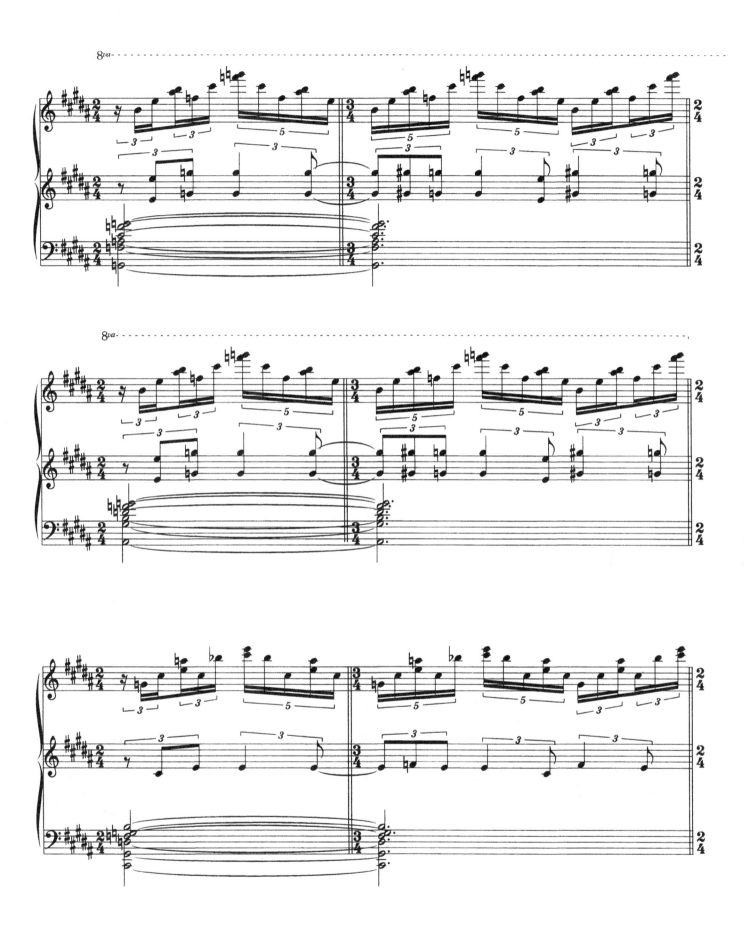

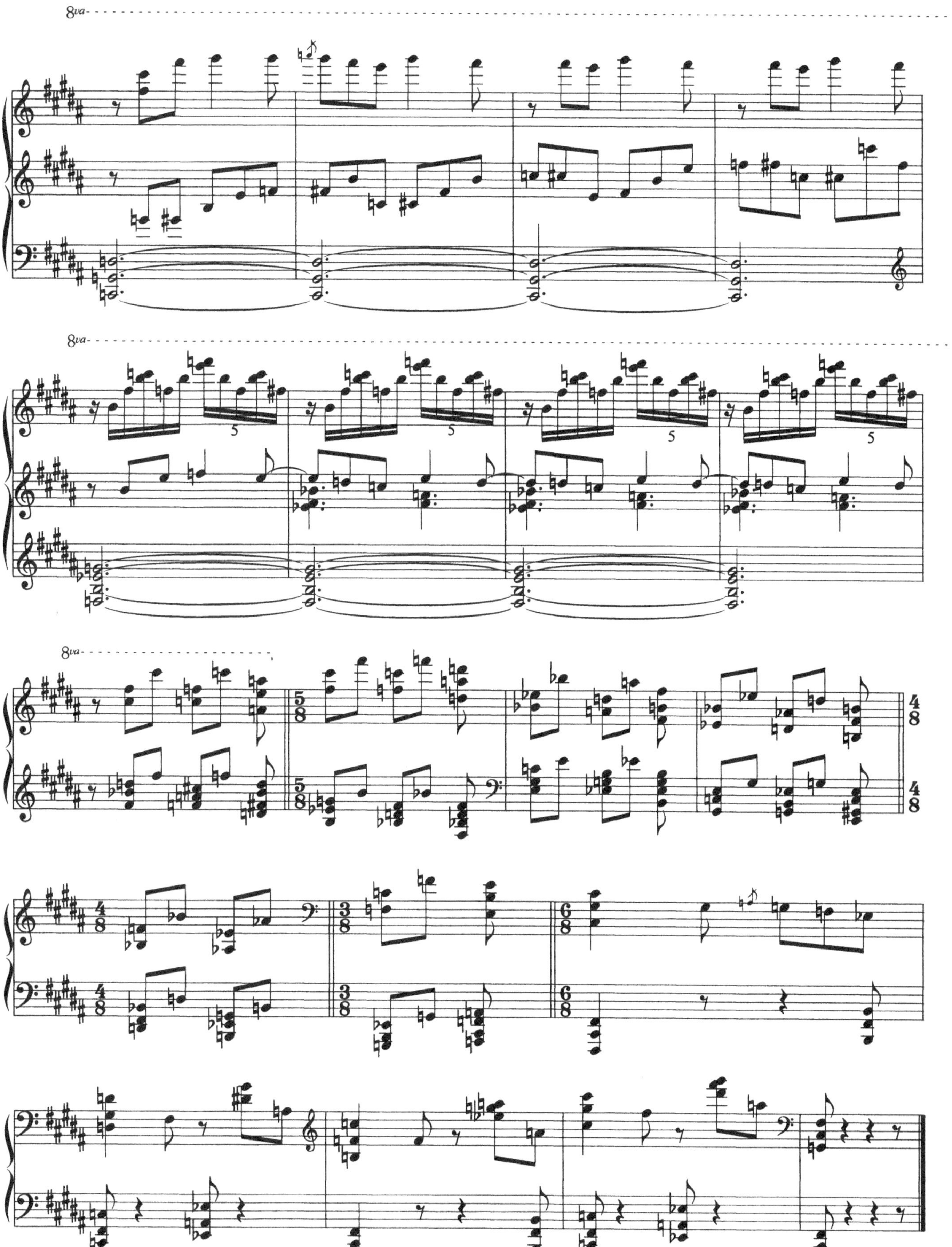
8va
8va
8va
5
5
5
5
5/8
4/8
3/8
6/8

A Long Remembered Sorrow

Leo Ornstein

Except for the section in B flat minor on pgs. 179–180, all accidentals apply only to those notes before which they stand. They do not carry through the measure.

176

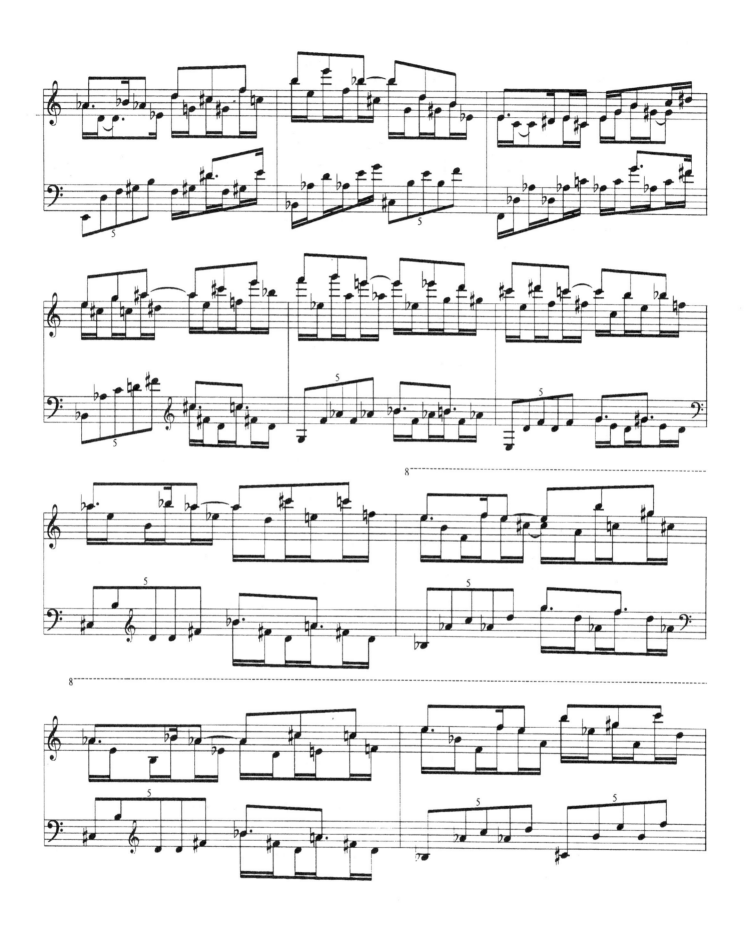

N.B. Upper beaming only for clarifying melodic line. Both hands should play simultaneously in eight equal subdivisions.

183

184

185

186

Metaphor No. 3

Leo Ornstein

198

Waltz No. 5

Leo Ornstein

All accidentals apply only to those notes before which they stand. They do not carry through the measure.

211

213

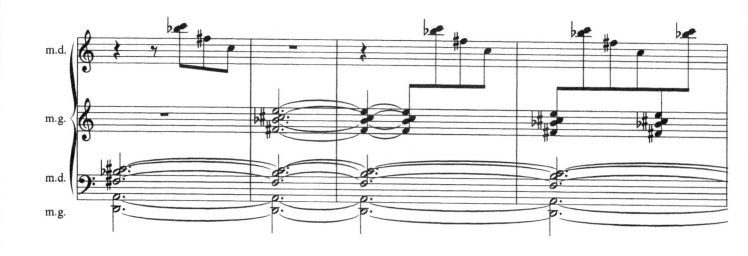

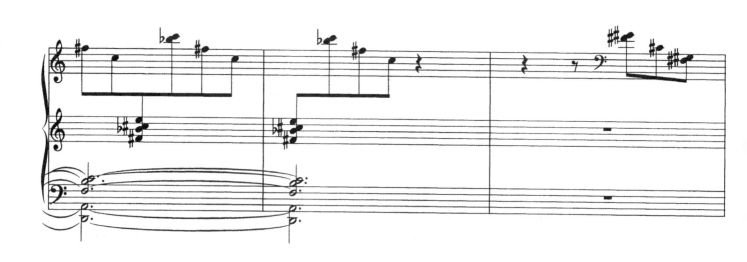

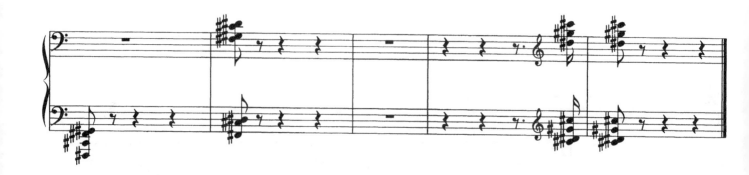

A Morning in the Woods

Leo Ornstein

217

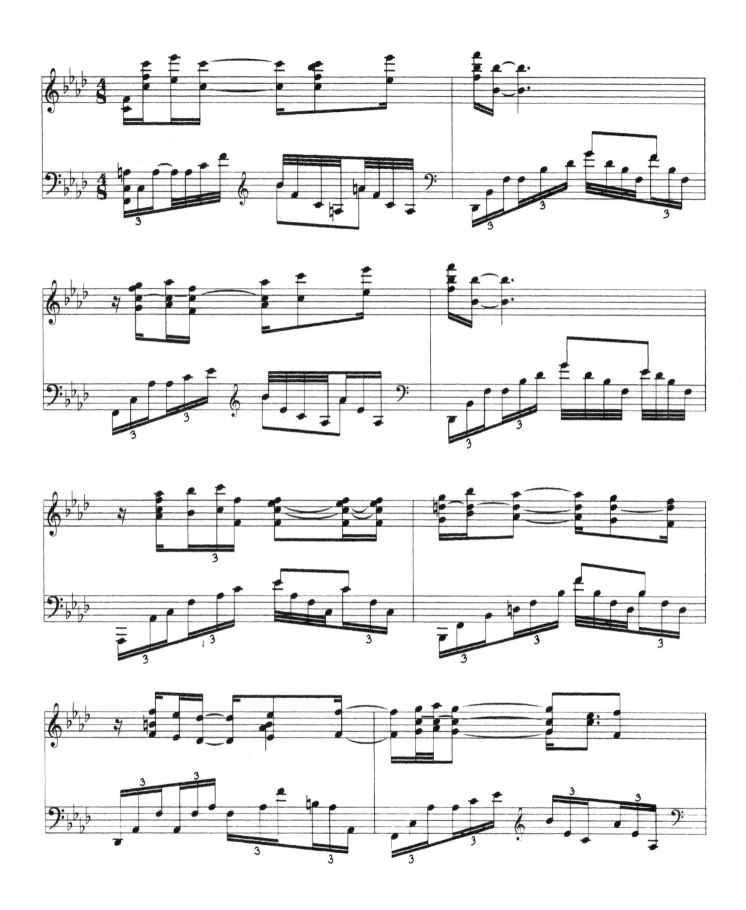

225

Waltz No. 12

Leo Ornstein

All accidentals apply only to those notes before which
they stand. They do not carry through the measure.

230

Waltz No. 9

Leo Ornstein

243

Piano Sonata No. 8

The composer makes the following observations:

"Perhaps I should amplify the Take Off that I introduce on Page 260 line 4."

"A rhythmic pattern, page 260 line 2, occurred to me and triggered the image of young dancers facing each other and improvising, whether consciously or unconsciously, some choreography of seemingly primitive origins. The nervous gyrations seemed incredible. The faces, glazed and showing almost no response to what they were doing, made me want to make some musical comment on the scene. The persistent bass is its own comment on the breathless scraps in the treble clef."

In reference to the second movement, he says:

"Some may object to the middle four Vignettes as an intrusion; others may find them a distinct contrast and relief from the brusqueness of the rest of the sonata."

1. Life's Turmoil and a Few Bits of Satire

Leo Ornstein

Throughout the first mvt. all accidentals apply only to those notes before which they stand. They do not carry through the measure.

248

250

255

Keep hammering away - This is obviously a take-off.

261

263

267

269

2. A Trip to the Attic—a Tear or Two for a Childhood Forever Gone

A. The Bugler

All four sections of the second movement use accidentals in the conventional manner in which they carry through the measure in the usual way.

272

B. A Lament For A Lost Toy

C. A Half Mutilated Cradle—Berceuse

D. First Carousel Ride and Sounds of a Hurdy Gurdy

278

279

Tempo I

3. Disciplines and Improvisations

Throughout the third movement, with the exception of the C# minor section on pages 293 and 294, all accidentals apply only to those notes before which they stand. They do not carry through the measure.

289